The Story of Abraham Lincoln

THE CHILDREN'S HEROES SERIES
Edited by John Lang

THE STORY OF
ABRAHAM LINCOLN

NEBRASKA
IOWA
COLORADO
KANSAS
Topeka
MISSOURI
St. Louis
Missouri R.
ILLINOISE
Chicago
Bloomington
Springfield
Alton
Salem
INDIANA
Gosport
OHIO
Ohio R.
KENTUCKY
Ft. Henry
Fort Donelson
Mason and Dixon's Line
OKLAHOMA
NEW MEXICO
INDIAN TERR.
ARKANSAS
TENNESSEE
Nashville
Shiloh
Corinth
Chattanooga
MISSISSIPPI
Vicksburg
Mississippi R.
ALABAMA
Mobile
Baton Rouge
New Orleans
LOUISIANA
TEXAS
MEXICO
GULF OF MEXICO
FLORIDA
GEORGIA
Atlanta
Savannah
S. CAROLINA
Columbia
Charleston
Ft. Sumter
NORTH CAROLINA
VIRGINIA
Richmond
WEST VIRGINIA
WASHINGTON
MD
Baltimore
Gettysburg
PENNSYLVANIA
New York
N.J.
Philadelphia
ATLANTIC
OCEAN
English Miles
0
100
200
Longitude West 90 from Greenwich
105
100
95
90
85
80
75
40
35
30
25

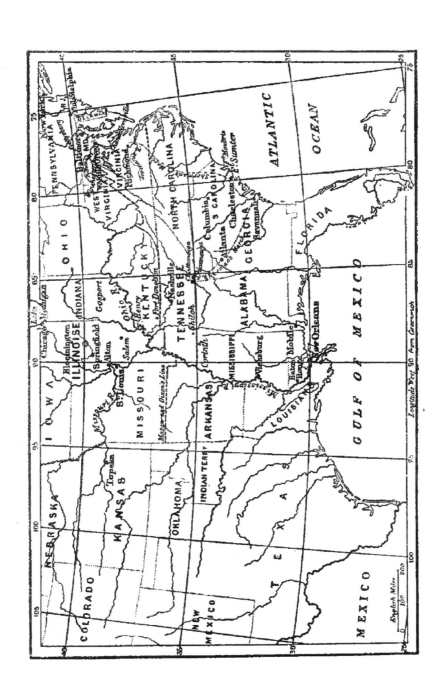

For the first time he saw negroes being scourged

THE STORY OF ABRAHAM LINCOLN

BY MARY A. HAMILTON
WITH PICTURES BY S. T. DADD

LONDON: T. C. & E. C. JACK
NEW YORK: E. P. DUTTON & CO.

TO
MARGOT

O CAPTAIN! MY CAPTAIN!

"O Captain! my Captain! our fearful trip is done!
The ship has weathered every rack, the prize we sought is won.
The port is near, the bells I hear, the people all exulting,
While follow eyes the steady keel, the vessel grim and daring;
        But O heart! heart! heart!
        O the bleeding drops of red,
          Where on the deck my Captain lies,
            Fallen cold and dead.

O Captain! my Captain! rise up and hear the bells;
Rise up—for you the flag is flung—for you the bugle trills,
For you bouquets and ribbon'd wreaths—for you the shores a-crowding:
For you they call, the swaying mass, their eager faces turning;
        Here Captain! dear father!
        This arm beneath your head!
        It is some dream that on the deck
            You've fallen cold and dead.

My Captain does not answer, his lips are pale and still,
My father does not feel my arm, he has no pulse nor will,
The ship is anchor'd safe and sound, its voyage closed and done,
From fearful trip the victor ship comes in with object won;
        Exult, O shores, and ring, O bells!
        But I with mournful tread
        Walk the deck; my Captain lies,
            Fallen cold and dead."

—*Walt Whitman.*

CONTENTS

Chapter	Page
I. Boyhood	1
II. The Young Backwoodsman	17
III. Slavery	30
IV. Lincoln the Lawyer	44
V. Defeat of the Little Giant	57
VI. The New President and Secession	73
VII. The War	84
VIII. Victory	100
IX. "O Captain! My Captain!"	110

LIST OF PICTURES

"For the first time he saw negroes being scourged"	*Frontispiece*
"The bullet passed right through his heart"	6
"Sometimes he did sums on the wooden shovel"	14
"His huge arms closed round Armstrong like a vice"	24
"Springing to his feet, he poured out what was in his mind"	58
Lincoln reading Emancipation Proclamation to his Cabinet	94
Lincoln discussing plan of campaign with General Grant	104
"Lincoln visited all the divisions of his army in turns"	110

THE STORY OF
ABRAHAM LINCOLN

CHAPTER I

BOYHOOD

IN this little book I am going to try to tell you something about Abraham Lincoln. There is far more to say about him than can be fitted into so small a space; and perhaps when you are older you will read about him for yourselves, and read his wonderful speeches.

The greatest names in American history are those of George Washington and Abraham Lincoln. These two men are great in the true sense of the word; they are great because they loved their country, purely and passionately, better than themselves, and gave their lives to its service. They thought nothing of their own honour and glory: to the last they were simple and true. Americans may well be proud of two such patriots; and from them every one may be glad to learn what real greatness means. Their work has made America what it is.

Less than forty years before Abraham Lincoln was born, America belonged to England. In the time of Charles I., numbers of people who loved freedom and hated the wrongful government of the king left their country and sailed to the New World. Samuel Lincoln was one of these men.

For a long time they were few in number. The greatest part of the country was unknown forest, inhabited by wild beasts, or vast plains which belonged to fierce tribes of Red Indians. Life for the early settlers was very hard and rough. They had to cut down trees to build their houses, and to kill wild animals to get their food. Nevertheless they soon grew to love the country where they lived, where they married and brought up their children; and their wild open life made freedom more precious to them than anything else. They began to resent the action of the English Government, which wanted to tax them to pay for wars which were agreed upon in the Parliament in London, where America had no voice to speak for her. On

July 4, 1776, in the reign of George III., the chief citizens met together and declared that America was a free united country, with a right to govern itself. The 4th of July—"Independence Day"—is the greatest day of all in America.

For seven years there was war. In this war Abraham's great-grandfather, John Lincoln, served as a soldier. The Americans were led by George Washington.

England was defeated, and America—the United States of America—was a free country. From this time on, America belonged to the Americans. But a great many years had to pass before they made of the country the America that we know. Now there are towns everywhere: you can get from one end to the other of the great country, far bigger than the whole of Europe, by trains that travel day and night from north to south and east to west. Then there were very few towns, most of them along the coast, and no railways. All the west was unknown.

After the war was over, bands of explorers set out to fight the Indians and to find new homes for themselves. And Abraham Lincoln's grandfather, after whom he was named, was one of the first of these explorers. He sold his little piece of land in Virginia, and tramped through the forests till he found a place to build a new home, carrying his youngest son Thomas on one shoulder, and with his loaded rifle in his other hand ready to shoot any Indian who should attack him. In Kentucky some white men had already settled and built a small fort; near it Lincoln cut down trees and built a hut for himself and his wife and his three sons to live in.

When Abraham was a small boy he used to listen to the stories which his father Thomas told of their life there in the constant fear of Indian attack. There was one story which Thomas told very often, the story of his father's death.

He was at work cutting down the trees, so as to clear an open space near the house which he could plough and then sow with seed.

One morning he set out as usual with his three boys. They were talking together as they walked, and none of them saw that behind one of the trees an Indian was hiding, his dark skin strangely painted with arrows and circles in white and scarlet, and on his head a tuft of black feathers standing upright and waving as he moved. In his hand he had a gun. As soon as the father had passed, the Indian came out from behind the tree, moving without making any sound. He shot at Abraham from behind, and the bullet passed right through his heart. The father fell down dead before the eyes of his sons. They were terrified. The two eldest ran off, one to the house and the other to the fort, to bring help. Thomas, the youngest, was only six. He could not run so fast as his brothers, and he was too much frightened to try. He stood still beside his father's body, not understanding what had happened. His eldest brother, Mordecai, made all speed to the house. As soon as he reached it he took down a gun, loaded it, and jumped up to the window so that he might shoot at the Indian out of it. As he looked out he saw the Indian walk up to the place where the dead body lay, look at it for a moment, then pick up little Thomas, put him under his arm, and turn to walk away with him. Mordecai felt his heart stand still with fear; but he was a brave boy, and his father had taught him how to shoot at a long distance. He aimed straight at the white star painted on the Indian's naked chest. There was an awful moment. Then the Indian fell back dead upon the ground, dropping the child from his arms. Thomas ran to the house as fast as his legs would carry him, screaming with fear, for now several other Indians began to appear from the wood. Mordecai fired again and again at them from the house; and people came from the fort, brought by his brother, and drove the Indians away.

Mordecai, when he grew up, spent his life in waging war upon the Indians, killing them wherever he met them. Thomas was neither so strong nor so clever as his brother. He became a carpenter, but he was never a very good carpenter. He was not very good at anything but sitting by the fire telling stories. He did that very well indeed, and people generally were fond of him; but he was not a successful person. He had none of his son's wonderful power of work; he always wanted to do something else, not the thing before him, and live somewhere else, not settle down to work where he was.

The bullet passed right through his heart

He built himself a log-cabin at Elizabethtown, on the edge of the forest, and when he was twenty-eight he got married and took his wife to live there.

It is said that all great men have had great mothers. Nancy Hanks had much more character than her husband, and her son was much more like her. She had a very sweet, unselfish nature, and every one loved her. She had had more education than her husband, and could read and write: she taught him to sign his name.

After their first child came—a daughter called Sarah—Thomas Lincoln, who always thought he could make a fortune somewhere else, moved farther west to a place called Nolin's Creek. The place was not at all attractive, but it was cheap. The soil was hard; it was rocky and barren, and nothing but weeds seemed to grow in it. Only a very energetic man could have made much out of it, and Thomas was not very energetic. They were very poor.

It was here, in an uncomfortable log-cabin, that his son Abraham was born, on the 12th of February 1809; and here he lived until he was seven.

The hut had only one room. It was very

roughly built. Stout logs had been laid on top of one another, then bound together with twigs, and the holes filled up with clay and grass and handfuls of dead leaves. There was no ceiling, only the log roof.

The two children climbed up a shaky ladder to a loft in the roof, where they slept on a bed of dry leaves, covered with an old deerskin, lying close together to keep themselves warm. As they lay there, they could count the stars that looked in through the spaces between the logs that made the roof. The windows had no glass; the door was only an opening over which a deerskin was hung as a curtain. In winter it was terrible. The wind blew in, icy cold; there was nothing to keep it out, except when sometimes the entrance was blocked up with snow, and no one could go out or come in until a pathway had been dug.

In the autumn the house used to be full of dead leaves that whirled about in the middle of the floor. The only comfort in the hut was the huge fire; it filled up nearly the whole of one side, and in front of it was a great bearskin rug. On this the two children spent the days in winter, playing together, or leaning against their mother's knee while she told them stories—fairy tales, or true stories about Indians and old American history, or parables from the Bible. In the winter you could not keep warm anywhere else; and in the autumn there were damp fogs that made it unwholesome outside, or heavy rains that came through the roof; the only thing to do was to get as near the fire as possible. Above it were ranged all the household pots and pans; the meat, a haunch of venison, or a couple of rabbits, hung from the roof. Cooking was very simple, for there was no choice of food: it consisted of game shot in the forest, or fish caught in the streams, roots and berries from the wood; bread was made of flour ground from Indian corn, which was the only thing that grew in the rough fields. Until he was a grown man Abraham had never tasted any other sort of bread.

The life was uncomfortable, often dangerous—for an Indian attack was possible at any time—and always the same. No visitors came to see the Lincolns; there were few friends for them to go and see, only the scattered settlers living in huts like their own.

Abraham very soon learnt to make himself useful. He would cut and bring home wood for the fire; help his mother in the house, or his father out-of-doors. In summer he spent long hours roaming about the woods. He soon learned to use a rifle, for it was not safe to go far unarmed, and he became a good shot. He remembered very little about this time when he grew older. One day he had been out fishing, and at the end of it he caught a single fish. With this he was walking home to supper, when he met a soldier. His mother had taught him he must always be good to soldiers, who fought for their country, and therefore the little boy gave the soldier his fish.

His father always thought that he should be better off somewhere else. He heard that across the Ohio River there was rich land which any one could have who chose to go and take it: so when Abraham was seven, and his sister nine, they moved. The father built a raft, and put his family and all the goods he had, after selling his house, on to it, and they sailed down the river, getting food on the way by shooting and fishing, till they came to a place they liked called

Little Pigeon Creek. It was simply an opening in the forest.

Here they disembarked, and for a year they lived in a roughly built shelter, without a floor or doors or windows, while the father and his son built a better cabin, and cut down trees and shrubs to clear a place for planting corn. When it was finished, Abraham's aunt and uncle, Mr. and Mrs. Sparrow, and two cousins, John and Denis Hanks, came to live with them. The three boys were great friends, and they worked together on the farm until they all grew up.

Abe, as they called him, was a very tall boy for his age: his long legs were always in his way, and they seemed to get longer every day. He never wore stockings until he was a young man, but moccasins, such as the Indians wear—shoes of leather, with a fringe round the top—and long deerskin leggings; a deerskin shirt which his mother had made him, and a cap which was seldom on his head, it being covered enough by his thick black hair. His hair was never tidy; always in his eyes, and having to be pushed back. Abe was clever with his axe, and a good workman; his mother had taught him to spell, but there was little chance of learning in Pigeon's Creek.

For a year the little family lived there very happily; then a mysterious sickness broke out in the place, no one knew why or how to cure it. They called it the milk sickness; many people fell ill of it, and hardly any one recovered. Mr. and Mrs. Sparrow both died of it in the autumn, and a few days afterwards Mrs. Lincoln sickened and died too. To her children this was a terrible grief. Abraham, though a boy when she died, never forgot his mother: she had taught him his first lessons, and from her came that sweetness of nature, that power of thinking first of others, that made every one who knew him love him. It was at the time of his mother's death that the sadness which never left him came upon him. In later life, people who really knew him said that, in spite of his fun and power of making other people laugh, he was the saddest man they ever knew.

A dreary winter followed. At the end of it Thomas Lincoln brought home a new wife to his little cabin. Sally Bush was a widow, with three children; she was a good and kind woman, and Abe really loved her and she him. She said afterwards that he had never all his life given her a cross word or look, or refused to do anything she asked him; that he was the best boy she had ever seen. He was indeed the sunshine of the house; but in many ways he was very lonely. He was hungry for knowledge, for books and teaching. All the schooling he ever had was a month now and then with a travelling teacher who passed through Pigeon's Creek on his way to somewhere else; but none of these teachers knew much beyond the three R's: one who knew Latin was regarded as a sort of magician. In all, he had not so much as one year at school, taught by five different teachers.

But Abe was not the sort of boy to learn nothing because there was nobody to teach him. He had a few books that had been his mother's, and he read them again and again until he knew everything that was in them. John Hanks, his cousin, says of him: "When Abe and I returned to the house from work, he would go to the cupboard, snatch a piece of corn-bread, take down a book, sit down, cock his legs as high as his head, and read." The Bible and "Pilgrim's Progress," "Æsop's Fables," and "Robinson

Crusoe," these were his books; he knew them by heart. In the intervals of work he used to tell them to his companions. He thought over every word until he understood it. In this way he learned more from a few books than many people do from whole libraries, because he learned to think. He questioned everything, and asked himself if he thought so too, and why he thought so.

One day he borrowed the life of George Washington from a farmer who lived near; as he lay in the loft he read it with eagerness. In the middle he was called away to work, and in the meantime the rain came in and ruined the book. Abraham went in despair to the farmer and told him what had happened. "Never mind," said the farmer. "You do three days' work for me for nothing and you may keep the book; I don't want it." To his joy he thus became possessed of a new treasure to be studied again and again. This book more than any other made him a patriot: he longed to get out into the great big world where he could serve his country. In the evenings he used to sit silent for hours, thinking. Sometimes he did sums of all sorts on the wooden shovel; making figures on it with

Sometimes he did sums on the wooden shovel

a piece of charcoal. When it was quite full he shaved off the top with his knife so as to have a clean slate in the morning.

All his companions liked Abe and admired him. He worked very hard, but farm work did not interest him; he liked dinner and play better; and sometimes he used to stop work and climb on to a gate or a dead tree-stump, and make absurd speeches or comic sermons to his companions, or recite passages from his favourite books.

They thought him a quaint fellow, with some strange ideas. One of these strange ideas was his tenderness to animals. He never cared much for sport, because it seemed to him cruel. He showed his tenderness to animals when quite a small boy. One day he was playing in the woods with a boy called John Davis. In their game they ran a hedgehog into a crevice between two rocks, and it got caught fast. For two hours they tried every sort of plan to get it out, but without any success. They were not able to pull it out, and it could not move itself. Abraham could not bear to leave the poor thing to die in pain. He ran off to the blacksmith's shop, quite a quarter of a mile away, and borrowed a pole with an iron hook fastened to the end; with this they were able to set the little animal free. This care for animals was only one sign of Abraham's tenderness of heart. All little children and old people trusted him and his word. He was very soon known as "Honest Abe."

CHAPTER II

THE YOUNG BACKWOODSMAN

FOR Abraham life was dull and very monotonous: the round of work was much the same, summer and winter. He longed to escape from the dull work of a farm labourer; to go out and see the world. Until he was twenty-one, however, he was bound to serve his father; and his father seems to have had no idea that his son was fit for anything better than ordinary farm work. Other people nevertheless were struck by Abraham.

Until he was nineteen he had not left home at all; but then one day a rich landowner who lived near came to him. He wanted some one to help his son to take a raft loaded with different kinds of goods down the Ohio River, selling the goods at the different places they passed. Abraham had struck this Mr. Gentry as being an honest and capable lad; he therefore asked him to undertake the voyage, and Abraham consented at once, glad of any chance of seeing something of life outside the settlement.

He took charge of the raft and steered it successfully down the river; the voyage took them past the great southern sugar plantations, right down to New Orleans. They had no adventures of any sort until they had almost come to New Orleans.

One night they encamped at Bâton Rouge, a place on the bank of the river. Here they fastened their raft, and lay down to sleep on it for the night, wrapped up in thick blankets. They were both sound asleep. Suddenly Abraham started up. He heard the sound of many soft footsteps all round him. In the darkness, at first, he could see nothing; then he became aware that a band of negroes was attacking the raft, ready to steal their goods and to murder them. Abraham's cry waked up his companion, young Allan Gentry, and they threw themselves upon the negroes. If Abraham had not been uncommonly strong and active they must both have lost their lives, for the negroes far outnumbered them. He seized a huge log of wood, which served him as a club, and brandished it in his hand. His great height and the unknown

THE YOUNG BACKWOODSMAN 19

weapon which he whirled round his head, terrified the negroes. He hit first one and then another on the head and threw them overboard, Allan Gentry helping. The fight was very fierce for a few moments, and then the negroes turned and fled. Abraham and Allan pursued them a long way into the darkness, but the thieves did not dare to return, though two men could not have held their own for long against such numbers.

The voyage ended successfully, and Abraham returned home for two more years. At the end of that time his father again moved. John Hanks had gone west to Illinois; he wrote to his uncle, praising the new country, and urging him to come there too. Thomas Lincoln was always ready to try something new: he sold his farm and his land to a neighbour. All the goods of the household were packed in a waggon drawn by oxen; the family walked beside it. They tramped for more than a week until they came to the new State; the journey was not easy. It was February. The forest roads were ankle-deep in mud; the prairie a mere swamp, very difficult for walking. They had to cross streams that were swollen into rivers by the rains.

At last they arrived. John Hanks had

chosen a plantation for them, and got logs ready for building the house. Abraham worked very hard, and helped his father and John Hanks to make a cabin; then, with his own hands, he ploughed fifteen acres of ground. When that was done he cut down walnut trees, split them, and built a high and solid fence which went right round his father's property.

Abraham lived in Illinois until he was made President of the United States. Once he was addressing a meeting there, years after this, and Denis Hanks marched in amid the shouts and applause of the crowd, carrying on his shoulder a piece of the railing that Abraham had made for his father. It is now in the Museum at Washington, kept as a national treasure. How little could Abraham himself or any one who knew him at this time, have dreamed that this rail-splitter was to be the greatest man in America.

The winter that followed was one of the most severe ever known in Illinois; it is always referred to as the winter of deep snow. When spring came at last, Abraham said good-bye to his father and mother, and went out into the world to make a livelihood for himself. His boyish days were over. He

THE YOUNG BACKWOODSMAN

was now twenty-one, and very tall and strong for his age. More than six feet four inches in height, he seldom met a man taller than himself. He is a great exception to the saying that all great men have been small—for example, Napoleon, Cæsar, Hannibal, Shakespeare. Abraham was very well built; it was not till he stood up among other men that you realised that he was head and shoulders taller than most of them.

In the ordinary sense of the word, he had had no education. He knew no language but his own, and that not very well at this time. When asked could he write, he replied, "Well, I guess I could make a few rabbit-tracks." He had taught himself all the arithmetic he knew. But he knew two things that are the most important that can be got from any training: how to think, and how to work. When he made clear to himself what it was right to do, he did it without talking about it, all his life.

His experience in taking Mr. Gentry's cargo down to New Orleans induced a merchant called Offutt to offer him another job of the same kind. Offutt was an adventurous sort of dealer, who did all kinds of business. He wanted some one to help him who had a head on his shoulders, and he soon saw that Lincoln had plenty of sense. He therefore engaged him, and Lincoln took his cousin, John Hanks, to help him. They did not make much money by the voyage, but Lincoln showed great skill in managing the raft.

On this trip Lincoln came for the first time really face to face with slavery. New Orleans was a great slave market, and they spent some time there. For the first time he saw negroes being sold in the open streets, chained together in gangs. For the first time, too, he saw negroes being beaten; fastened to a block and scourged till the blood ran from their backs. Every one took it all as a matter of course, but Lincoln was deeply struck. His heart bled. At the time he said nothing, but he was silent for a long while afterwards, thinking over what he had seen. There and then, as his cousin used to tell afterwards, slavery ran its iron into him: to see these men chained was a torment to him, and he never forgot it: the picture was printed on his memory never to be forgotten, only to be wiped out when there were no more slaves in America. He was often in the slave states after this; but slavery always seemed to him horrible.

THE YOUNG BACKWOODSMAN 23

Offutt was quite satisfied with the way in which the young backwoodsman had managed the trip. After his return he offered him a post in his grocery store at New Salem. He had a kind of half shop, half office, with a mill behind it; here he sold everything that any one could want to buy—grocery, drapery, stationery, miscellaneous goods of all kinds. Lincoln was clerk, superintendent of the mill, and general assistant.

Offutt soon began to admire his assistant immensely. He declared that Lincoln was the cleverest fellow he knew—he could read, and talk like a book; he was so strong and active that he could beat any one at running, jumping, or wrestling. Lincoln did not know any one in New Salem, and this "wooling and pulling," as he called it, of Offutt's annoyed him a good deal; as he knew, it was not at all likely to make people like him. The young fellows of the place did not mind his supposed cleverness; they knew nothing about that, and cared nothing; but they did resent the idea that he was stronger than they were.

At first they did nothing: he looked rather a dangerous person to attack, and not at all likely to take things meekly. Offutt's loud and continual praise, however, was more than they could stand. As Lincoln was on his way home one evening a group of the strongest fellows in New Salem, the "boys of Clary's Grove," attacked him. Jock Armstrong, the biggest and burliest of them all, challenged him to a "wrastle." Jock was not as tall as Lincoln, but he was much more solidly built, with huge shoulders like an ox and immensely strong arms: no one in New Salem had ever been able to throw him, and he expected an easy victory over this strange clerk.

But Abe was as strong and as skilful as Jock: though he was thin his muscles were made of iron; his huge arms closed round the burly fellow like a vice. Even when his companions came to the champion's rescue Abe was a match for them. Armstrong was a sportsman and not ashamed to take a beating: he admired a man who was able to throw him. After this Lincoln had no stauncher friend, and he soon grew to be a person of importance in New Salem. His strength and his honesty made him respected.

Of his honesty there are numberless stories. One evening he was making up his accounts for the day. While doing so he found that he had charged a woman, who

His huge arms closed round Armstrong like a vice

THE YOUNG BACKWOODSMAN

had come in in the morning to buy a great number of little things, $6\frac{1}{4}$ cents—that is, about 3d.—too much. Until it was time to shut up the shop the money seemed to burn in his pocket. It was late when the time for locking up came, but he could not wait. He started off at once for the woman's house, though it was several miles off, and walked there and back in the darkness to pay her her 3d. before he went to bed. He knew he could not sleep until he had done so.

People trusted him: those who were in trouble soon found out how wise and gentle he was, and they went to him for advice and help. He had a wonderful way of quite forgetting himself, and only thinking of making other people happy: generally silent, he could tell stories so that every one laughed. But though he enjoyed talking and going to see people, he always worked very hard.

And he did not only work in the shop: he was always eager to learn more. After the day's task was done, he would walk miles to get hold of some book that he wanted, and read it on the way home. When his cousin, a lazy fellow, wrote to ask his advice, he replied: "What is wrong with you is your habit of needlessly wasting time: go to work; that is the only cure for your difficulty."

When he came to New Salem he met people who had been well educated, and he was at once struck by the difference between their way of speaking and his. He resolved to learn to speak correctly. One evening he walked to Kirkham and back — it was twelve miles away — and bought a grammar there. For the next few weeks he spent all his spare time in studying it: he used to sit with his feet on the mantelpiece and work for hours without moving. In this way he soon knew all there was to know about grammar. When you read his speeches you will find that they are written in English as beautiful and simple as that of the Bible, which was the book he knew best of all.

He only remained with Offutt for a year. Offutt was too fond of talking to make his business a success, and he had to give up the store. It was Lincoln's first attempt at earning his living, and learning a trade did not seem very successful. Instead of at once looking for some new work of the same sort he enlisted as a soldier. The State of Illinois was thrown into a state of wild excitement by an attack made at this

THE YOUNG BACKWOODSMAN 27

time by a powerful Indian tribe. Black Hawk crossed the Mississippi at the head of an army of red warriors. To drive them back, the Government of the country called for volunteers, and Abraham, who was one of the first to offer himself, was made a captain. The men entered for three months, during which they did a great deal of skirmishing and marching about, but took part in no regular battles. At the end of the time most of them went back to work. Abraham enlisted again; this time as a private in a battalion of scouts. He was not present at any battle, but he learnt something of war and a good deal of soldiers; it was hard work and not much glory. By the autumn Black Hawk was captured, and the war was at an end. Lincoln's horse had been stolen, and he had to walk back to New Salem, a three days' tramp. His campaigning had not been a great success.

When he returned, the elections for members of the Illinois Parliament were going on, and he offered himself as a candidate; spending the ten days between his return from the war and the time of election in making speeches. In New Salem he was popular, but he was not yet well known even there; he was young, and had had no experience. He was not elected, but he made good friends at the election time, and he began to be a capital speaker.

Meetings were not very formal in those days. One day when Lincoln was addressing a large hall full of people, in the middle of his speech he saw that a ruffian in the crowd was attacking a friend of his; they were struggling together, and his friend seemed to be having the worst of it. Lincoln jumped down from the platform where he stood, and marched to the middle of the room. He picked up the ruffian in his mighty arms and threw him some ten feet, so that he fell right outside the hall. There he lay, and did not attempt to return. Lincoln came back on to the platform and went on with his speech, just as if nothing had happened.

After the election he thought of becoming a blacksmith. Instead of this, he joined with a man called Berry in buying a store. Berry was a stupid and not very honest man. He got into debt; then he took to drinking, and soon afterwards died, leaving Lincoln with the business ruined and a lot of debts to pay.

After this he did not try storekeeping again: he was made postmaster of New Salem. This meant very little work: few people wrote letters there: he could carry the whole post in his hat, and he read every newspaper that came. He now had plenty of time for reading, and he read ceaselessly. Most of all, he read American history. The "Life of Washington" had been his earliest treasure; and as a boy he had pored over an old copy of the statutes of Indiana. This was, perhaps, the beginning of his interest in law. Now he was in a town, though a small one, and it was possible to get hold of books. He used to lie on his back under a tree, with his feet high up against the trunk, only moving so as to keep in the shade, and laying down the book now and then to think over what he had read and make sure that he understood it.

He studied surveying in this way for six weeks, and John Calhoun, the surveyor of the county, was so much astonished by his knowledge that he made him his assistant. His reading in law and history deepened his interest in politics: nothing interested him so much. He was resolved sooner or later to get into Parliament. One failure could not make him despair. There was a great world outside, and the door into Parliament was the door into that world. He was resolved to make his way in.

CHAPTER III

SLAVERY

IT would be a great mistake to think that Abraham Lincoln won success easily.

Looking back over the lives of great men, one is apt to think "How fortune helped them;" "What astonishing luck they must have had;" when one knows the end, it seems certain from the beginning. But when you know more about any one really great man, you are sure to find that he has risen only by endless hard work, and by knowing from the beginning what he wanted to be and do, and thinking only of that.

Success is never easy, and for Lincoln the path to it was a hard and uphill way. You have seen in what difficulties his life began: how he taught himself everything he learned, and made for himself every penny that he possessed. His first effort to get into Parliament, like his first efforts to make a living, seemed a failure. But this did not make him despair. Other people had risen, and he was going to rise. He was sure of one thing, that there is always plenty of room at the top, and he meant to reach the top. There is always a place for a man of strong purpose, who is honest, and who can think for himself. If a man really wants to serve his country, nothing need prevent him from doing it. And Lincoln saw that the first step to serving your country well is to be a good workman, a good friend, and a good citizen of your own town.

When the next election came he stood again, and this time he was elected; and after his two years of service came to an end, he was elected again. For eight years he was a member of the Parliament of his own State of Illinois; then, after four years away from politics, he was made member of Congress—that is, of the American Parliament, to which the States send representatives.

To be in Parliament was to be in touch with the big world; to have a share in the settlement of big questions. In the Illinois Parliament, Lincoln met a great many clever men; men who rose to important posts later. Few of them suspected that this tall, awkward, country-looking young lawyer, who did not speak much, but could tell such extraordinarily funny stories when he chose, was going to rise to be American President, to prove himself greater than any American of their time. Most of the members were small lawyers like himself. They were sent to Parliament because they were men in whom their fellow-citizens had confidence. They were honest men, but few of them had any more knowledge of politics than Lincoln himself.

The State of Illinois was very new, and its affairs had not yet become complicated. Lincoln soon learnt the ins and outs of parliamentary business; and he only found one man who was a better speaker than himself. This was a man with whom he was to have a great deal to do all his life; a man already well known in politics, and followed by a large party.

His name was Stephen Arnold Douglas. He was two years younger than Lincoln; like him he had been brought up in the rough surroundings of the West, where he had gone as a boy. His father was poor, but he was a gentleman. Well educated himself, he had given his son a good education of a sort.

When he was twenty-one Douglas became a lawyer. Very soon he became the foremost barrister in North Illinois, and soon entered the State Parliament. In the year of Lincoln's election he had been made Secretary of State; he was therefore a person of importance. Douglas was extremely clever; as a boy he learnt things quickly, and remembered them easily, unlike Lincoln, who learnt very slowly; he had a wonderful power of speech: he was ready and able to speak on any subject, and, even if he really knew very little about it, he always gave people the impression that he knew everything. He used to tell people what they wanted to hear, whereas Lincoln had a way of speaking the truth whether it was pleasant or not.

Douglas was very popular: he understood how to rule men, and he was intensely ambitious. Ambition was the strongest feeling in his heart; and his ambition was for himself: he dreamed already of being President of the United States. He was a short, thickly-built man; but it was the smallness of his mind, his selfish aims, that made Lincoln say that Douglas was the least man that he had ever met: he seemed to "Honest Abe" to care not at all for what he said or did, so long as his own success was safe; success was his one object.

It was an ambition very different from Lincoln's. Indeed, Lincoln was unlike any of the members whom he met: his aims were quite different from theirs. He looked to a future beyond himself. He did not think of his own success. What he wanted to attain by success was the power to help his country. Patriotism was his first and strongest feeling, and his patriotism was of the truest kind. He did not want to make America great because she ruled over a vast extent of territory: such greatness did not appeal to him at all. He wanted her to be great in the sense that she really lived up to the ideal set before her for ever in the Declaration of Independence—the ideal of a union of free men governing themselves well.

And Lincoln's ideals were real to him: in every question he was guided by his patriotism. He did not mind saying what he thought, whether people liked him for it or not: they must like him for what he was, and not for what he said, and unless they loved what was right, their liking was not worth having. When, after long thinking, he came to see what he thought the truth on any subject, he spoke out so that every one who heard must understand: he never said one thing and meant another, as Douglas did: he was as honest in his thoughts as in his actions.

Now in American politics there was one great question, more important than every other, the question of slavery. Cautious politicians, men with an eye to their own success, thought that this question had better be left alone. Really thoughtful men, men like Lincoln, saw that this question could not be left alone for ever. Some day, and the sooner the better, it must be settled. Anyhow, it was every honest man's duty to say what he thought. It is difficult now to realise quite what slavery meant. Perhaps you have read or heard of a book called "Uncle Tom's Cabin." It was written about this time by an American lady, who wanted to make all Americans see what slavery did mean—how terrible it could be.

If you drew a line across America just south of Lincoln's State of Illinois, slavery did not exist in the Northern States; it did exist in all the Southern States. Whenever the question was discussed, most people from the North thought it rather a bad thing, some thought it a very bad thing; people from the South all thought it was a good, or at least, a necessary, thing. They all agreed as a rule in thinking that, whether it was a good thing or a bad thing, there it was, and there was no good discussing it.

The real wrong lay far back in the past. Centuries ago, merchants had brought negroes over from Africa, and sold them in America as slaves.

As is always the case, when once the wrong had been brought in, when the evil had begun, it was almost impossible to get rid of it when people had grown used to it. When people could buy slaves who did not cost very much to do work for them, they did not want to do it themselves, especially if the work was disagreeable. They began to believe that black men were intended by nature to do all the disagreeable things. English merchants made great fortunes by bringing slaves to America; and the English Government supported them. And when, after the war, America was a free country, the Union of States which made it so was half composed of States that held slaves. These slaves were most valuable property. The men who drew up the Constitution,

George Washington and Thomas Jefferson and Alexander Hamilton, declared in it, "All men are free and equal: all men possess rights, which no one can take away from them." The Northern States gave up their slaves, and decided that slavery was illegal: the Southern States did not. They refused to join the Union unless they were allowed to keep their slaves. Now of course it was absurd to call a country free where slavery existed, or to say that all men have rights when millions of black men had no rights at all.

To the Southerner a black man was not a man, but a piece of property.

But it would not be quite fair to think that the Northerners who gave up slaves had always more lofty ideas than the Southerners. You must remember that slaves were much more useful in the South than in the North. The climate of the North was cold, and the work not of the sort that could be well done by untrained negroes. In the South it was so hot that it was difficult for white men to work, and work on the plantations needed no special skill.

At the time when the Declaration of Independence was drawn up and signed, one thing seemed to every American more important than anything else: that the country should be united in one whole. North and South must join together; no difference could outweigh a common nationality. The Southerners would not join the Union unless they were allowed to keep their slaves: therefore the Northerners left slavery in the South. They hoped, however, that it would gradually die out; and therefore a law was passed which declared that after twenty years no more slaves were to be brought from Africa.

When Southerners declared, as they very often did, that slaves were very well treated, that they were much happier and more comfortable than if they were free, this was true to a certain extent. Those slaves who were employed in the houses and gardens of their masters, those who were used as servants, were often very well treated. But however well they were treated, it is wrong for a man to have other men entirely in his power; wrong for him, and wrong for them. And although some masters did not abuse their power, some did—and all could, if ever they wanted to—without feeling that they were doing anything wrong. A white gentleman could beat his black slave to death if he chose; he would not be punished any more than if he beat a dog to death, and his friends would still think him a gentleman. Moreover, far the greater number of the slaves were not used as servants, but used as labourers on the cotton plantations. Here they were under the charge of an overseer. His one idea was to get as much work out of them as possible. They worked all day, and at night were often herded together in any sort of shed.

After Eli Whitney, a young American, invented a machine called the cotton gin, by using which one negro could pick twenty times as much cotton in a day as before, the business of working the cotton plantations with slaves made the Southern landowners very rich. Slaves were cheap: in a few days they made as much for their masters as they cost them, and their masters could make them work as hard as they liked. They were quite ignorant: their masters taught them nothing; they had no way of escape; they were absolutely at the mercy of the overseer with his whip. The masters came to regard these black fellow-beings simply as property: not so valuable as a horse, rather more useful than a dog;

they often forgot that they had any feelings. Children were sold away from their parents; a husband was sent to one plantation, and his wife to another. They were sometimes beaten for the smallest fault. If they tried to escape, bloodhounds were used to hunt them down. Dealers led them about in chains, and sold them in the public market exactly like animals. People who came from the North to the South, as Abraham Lincoln did, on his trip down the Ohio, and saw how the slaves were treated, were often shocked; but in the South people were used to it.

North of a certain line, slavery did not exist. Slaves used sometimes to run away from their masters and escape across this line; but in every Northern State there was a law, that escaped slaves had to be handed back to their master if he claimed them. The masters used to offer a reward to any one who handed back to them the body of their slave, alive or dead. This led to all sorts of difficulties, because in the Northern States a great many free negroes lived. Very often some one who was eager for the reward would capture an innocent free negro and hand him over to the master, declaring that he answered to the description of the missing slave. The question as to whether he was, or not, was decided not in the Northern State where he had been captured, but in the Southern State where the master lived, and no Southern court could be trusted to decide fairly in a case between a white man and a black.

Gradually this injustice roused a small party in the North, which openly declared that slavery was an abominable thing, and ought not to exist in America. The Abolitionists, as they called themselves, said that it was a disgrace to a free country that slavery should exist in it; that as long as it did exist, the Declaration of Independence had no meaning. Slavery ought to be abolished.

When Abraham Lincoln was about twenty-one, a paper called *The Liberator* began to appear. It was edited by a great man called William Lloyd Garrison. Its object was to rouse people to see the evils of slavery, and to get it made illegal. The Abolitionists were few in number, and very unpopular. They had to suffer for their beliefs in the North as well as in the South. The offices where *The Liberator* was printed were attacked by mobs of furious people, who burst in at the doors, broke every pane of glass in the windows, destroyed the printing press, and threw the type into the river. In St. Louis, William Lloyd Garrison was dragged round the town with a rope round his waist, while crowds of angry people hooted and hissed, spat at him, and threw rotten eggs and stones at his head. He only just escaped death. Many of his followers were murdered in the open streets. Even in Illinois, an innocent preacher, who had sympathised with them, was thrown into the river and drowned.

The Southern States were roused to fury. In the North, even sensible people who did not like slavery thought it very unwise to say anything against it. Slavery was a fact—it was no good to discuss it. Several Northern States sent petitions to Parliament, declaring their opinion that it was very unwise to discuss Abolition.

In Illinois, this was the view taken by nearly all Lincoln's friends. Lincoln did not agree with them. He thought the Abolitionists very often unwise; nothing, he saw, could be more dangerous than to rouse the feeling of the South: but nothing could make him seem to approve of slavery.

For Lincoln to see that any action was right, and to do it, was the same thing. He and one other man, called Stone, sent in a protest to the Illinois Parliament; in it they declared that they believed slavery to be founded upon injustice and upon bad policy. Lincoln spoke because he must. He had seen what slavery meant, and he hated slavery. But he saw that the South would not allow slavery to be abolished: if the North tried to do it, the country would be divided into two halves. He was not ready to face that. His love for his country came before everything. Everything must be borne, rather than that it should be divided.

The Abolitionists were a small party; and for the next seventeen years, the question of slavery was left as it was, as far as Parliament was concerned. During these seventeen years, Lincoln was perpetually turning it over in his mind; thinking and reading about it, and helping other people to think about it too.

CHAPTER IV

LINCOLN THE LAWYER

TWO years after Lincoln entered the Illinois Parliament, its meetings, which had been held at Vandalia, were transferred to Springfield. In Springfield Lincoln lived for the next five-and-twenty years, until he left it to go to Washington as President of the United States. Springfield was a country town, which thought itself rather important. The people paid a good deal of attention to dress; they gave evening parties of a quiet sort, where they played cards and talked politics. The business of the most prominent persons in the town was law. Almost all the members of Parliament were lawyers.

Lincoln found that his surveying did not occupy his time, or bring in a very large income; he had studied law-books, and knew very nearly as much as most of the young barristers of Springfield. Major Stuart, under whom he had served in the war against Black Hawk, took him into partnership. The partnership was not very successful. Lincoln was rather ignorant, and Stuart was too much occupied with his duties as member of Congress — the American Parliament—to teach him much.

After four years Lincoln left Stuart and joined another friend, Judge Stephen D. Logan. Logan had made Lincoln's acquaintance at the time of his first unsuccessful candidature for the Illinois Parliament. He had then greatly admired the young man's pluck and good sense, and the cheerful way in which he accepted his defeat. Later, he had been struck by the sound reasoning of his political speeches. Logan himself was not only a first-rate lawyer, he was a man of wide education and culture: Abraham learned more than law from him. Even after Lincoln left the partnership, and set up an office of his own, the two men remained close friends.

Although busy during the winter in Parliament, Lincoln worked very hard at his business. He knew that no one can succeed in anything without hard work, and he saw that to become a really good lawyer would help him in politics, and make him a more useful citizen of the

State. Moreover, he understood, more clearly than most men have done, that every deed in life is connected to every other; no man can escape the consequences of what he is and does. Every act and every speech is important.

Lincoln was four times elected to the Illinois Parliament—that is, he sat in it for eight years. For four years — between 1845-49 — he was member for Illinois in Congress. In Congress he spoke and voted against the war that was being waged against Mexico. The aim of the war was the conquest of Texas and California. The South urged this because they wanted the number of slave-owning States to be equal to the number of free States. They were always afraid that new States would be created out of the undeveloped territory in the North-West; and, if this were to happen, the slave States would be in a minority in Congress. If Texas were added as a slave State, the slave States would have a majority of one: there would be fourteen free and fifteen slave States. The Northern members, for the most part, did not see the point; they did not unite against the Southern demands; and consequently the South succeeded. In the war

Mexico was defeated, and Texas was added to the Union.

At the end of his last year of membership, 1849, Lincoln applied for a post in the Government office. Why he did so it is difficult to understand, for it would have put an end to his political career, as officials may not sit in the House. Fortunately his request was refused.

He returned to his home in Springfield, where he lived in a big, plain house, painted a dirty yellow, with a big piece of untidy garden behind, and a small field at the side. He had married seven years before, and had now three sons. He was devoted to these boys, and used to play all sorts of games with them, as they grew bigger.

For the next five years he devoted himself mainly to his work as a lawyer. He was now forty years of age. In Springfield and everywhere in Illinois he was admired, respected, and loved. But the high opinion of other people never made him easily satisfied with himself. To the end of his life he never stopped working and learning. He now resolved to become a really good lawyer. He knew that in law he could learn the art of persuading people, and of expressing clearly what he wanted to say. To help in this he took up the study of mathematics with extraordinary energy. Examining his own speeches, he seemed to find in them some confusion of thought. To make his own ideas clear, and to be sure that he expressed them clearly and truly, and never conveyed to others an impression that was not true, he bought a text-book of Euclid. The first six books of this he learnt by heart. He said "I wanted to know what was the meaning of the word 'demonstrate.' Euclid taught me what demonstration was."

After a year or two Lincoln was regarded as the equal of any lawyer in Springfield. He had one weakness, however. If he did not believe in the justice of his case, or if he thought the man for whom he had to speak was not quite honest, he did not defend well. His friend Judge Davis says, "A wrong cause was poorly defended by him."

A story is told of a man who came to Lincoln's office and asked his help in getting six hundred dollars from a poor widow. Lincoln listened to the man and then said, "Yes, there is no reasonable doubt but I can gain your case for you. I can set a whole neighbourhood at loggerheads. I can distress a widowed mother and her six fatherless children, and thereby get for you six hundred dollars which rightfully belong, as it appears to me, as much to them as it does to you. I advise you to try your hand at making six hundred dollars some other way."

Every one in Springfield valued "Honest Abe's" opinion. All sorts of people brought their troubles to him. His sympathy and his tenderness of heart made them trust him. He was one of the people; he never felt himself above them. To the end of his life he did not grow proud, and he was never ashamed of his early poverty. When he was President he told some of his friends of a dream he had had, which might very well have been true. He dreamt that at some big public meeting he was walking through the hall up to the platform, from which he was going to speak. As he passed, a lady sitting at the end of one of the rows of seats said to another sitting next her, so loudly that he could hear: "Is that Mr. Lincoln? Why, he looks a very common sort of person!" "I thought to myself in my dream," said Lincoln, "that it was true, but that God Almighty seemed to prefer common people, for He had made so many of them."

Nothing in Lincoln is more truly great than his power of seeing the value of common things and common people. He knew that the things which appeal to men as men, which are common to humanity, are the most valuable of all. He counted on this when he abolished slavery. Freedom is a right common to all men; and there is somewhere in every one an instinct which knows that it is wrong to make other people do things which are too disagreeable to do yourself.

During these years at Springfield, Abraham read a great deal. Shakespeare and Burns were his favourite poets: he knew Shakespeare better than any other book except the Bible. He read and thought unceasingly about politics, and he talked about them with his friends. The history of America he studied until he knew everything there was to know. Above all, he thought about slavery. Events were taking place which made it plain that the question of slavery could not be left where it was. It was no longer possible to act as if the difference between North and South did not exist.

As years went on the difference became more and more plain. The North, which had been poor and barren, only half cultivated by ignorant and uneducated settlers, was growing richer than the prosperous lazy

South. Workmen came to the North from all parts of the world: poor men with good brains and strong arms, ready and able to work intelligently, to improve the land, to make wheat grow where stones and bushes had been. None of these men went to the South, for there work was done by slaves so cheaply that no paid worker had a chance. But the difference between the intelligent labour of free men working for themselves, and the mechanical labour of slaves working for their masters, soon began to tell.

In the North schools sprang up everywhere: the people became better and better educated. Men who had grown up in the backwoods, like Abraham Lincoln, taught themselves, and rose to be lawyers and statesmen by their own efforts; others who had had the chance of being taught, did the same. It was possible for any man of brains to rise from the bottom to the top. Inventions were made which enabled all kinds of new work to be done and new wealth produced. The North was rich in material: richer in the men she had to work it, who were helped and encouraged by the freedom which threw every career open to real talent.

In the South all power was in the hands of the aristocratic families, who had had it always. The work was done by slaves: owners did not want to educate their slaves, for then they were afraid that they would want their freedom. The coal mines of the South were not discovered; they could not have been worked by slaves. The South began to be very jealous of the North, and the North began to disapprove of the South. More and more people began to see that slavery was wrong: people were not yet ready to say that slavery ought to cease to be, but they were ready to say that it must not be extended.

At the time of the Mexican war the South had shown that it wanted to extend slavery. This frightened the North. In 1850 an agreement was made, known as the Missouri Compromise. By this a line (36°30'), called Mason and Dixon's line, was drawn across the map of America. North of this line, slavery was never to exist. Speakers on both sides declared that the Missouri Compromise was as fixed as the Constitution itself. Stephen Arnold Douglas was the loudest in expressing this opinion. "It is eternal and fundamental," he declared.

Douglas was a trader of the great party known as the Democrats. He held that the people of every State had a right to decide questions affecting that State, and not the Central American Government.

Douglas had one great aim, which was to him far more important than any question of political right or wrong: he wanted to be made President. To secure this, he saw that he must get the support of the South. To win the support of the South, he took a most dangerous and important step: one which was the immediate cause of the war which broke out six years later. He declared that the people of any state or territory could decide whether or not they would have slavery in their State: they could establish it or prohibit it.

He went further than this. Two new territories had been organised in the north-west—Nebraska and Kansas. They claimed to be admitted to the Union as States. Both States were, of course, north of Mason and Dixon's line, and therefore by the Missouri Compromise they must be free States. But the South was bent on creating new slave States as fast as the North could create free States: they wanted to make Kansas a slave State. Stephen Douglas therefore introduced, in 1854, the famous Kansas-Nebraska Bill. It declared that Kansas might be slave-holding or free, as the people of the territory should decide.

The result of this Bill was for the first time to unite together a strong party in the North in opposition to the Democrats, who were allied to the South. This new party called itself Republican. Lincoln was a spokesman of their views. They declared, firstly, that Congress, which is the Parliament representing all the States which together formed the Union, has the right to decide whether slavery shall be lawful in any particular State or not, and not the people of that State alone. Secondly, they declared that, in the case of Kansas, Congress had already, four years ago, decided that Kansas could not have slavery, because it lay beyond the line, north of which slavery could not exist. Resolutions were passed in many of the Northern State Parliaments against the Kansas-Nebraska Bill. The Parliament of Illinois sent one.

Now it was quite clear to keen-sighted politicians that, while Douglas and his party pretended that they wanted to give the people of Kansas the choice between owning slaves and not doing so, what they really wanted was to force Kansas to have slaves. Those who supported the Missouri Congress declared that it was illegal to give Kansas the choice however she used it.

Events soon proved that Kansas was not to have any choice at all. Kansas had few inhabitants; but the opinion of the people of the State was against slavery. Next door to Kansas, however, on the east, was the slave-holding State of Missouri. From Missouri bands of armed men came into Kansas in order to vote for slavery at the election and to prevent the real voters from using their votes against it. Free fighting went on in the State. An election was held at which armed men kept away those who would have voted for freedom, and a pro-slavery man was chosen. But few of the people of Kansas had been allowed to vote. The free party met at another place afterwards, and a genuine popular vote elected an anti-slavery man. Civil war went on in Kansas for two years.

Now the importance of these events is this. Up till now most people in the North had believed that slavery ought to be left alone, because it would gradually die out. The Kansas-Nebraska Bill and the Kansas election made it perfectly clear that the South was not going to let slavery die out; on the contrary, they wanted to spread it to strengthen themselves against the North.

Douglas was member for Chicago, in the

north of Illinois. He came down to Illinois to win the State to his views, and made a series of speeches there. This at once called Lincoln to the fore. He saw more clearly, perhaps, than any man in America what the Kansas Bill meant. It meant that either North and South must separate, as the Abolitionists—that is, the party which held that slavery ought to cease to be—and some people in the South hoped; or that the North would have to force the South to abandon the attempt to spread slavery. He made a series of great speeches in Illinois, in which he made it quite clear that Douglas and his followers, and the men of the South, might say that they wanted to leave States free to have slavery or not as they chose, but what they really desired was to force them to have slavery whether they chose or not. "This declared indifference, but, as I must think, covert real zeal for the spread of slavery, I cannot but hate: I hate it because of the monstrous injustice of slavery itself... I say that no man is good enough to govern another man without that man's consent. Slavery is founded upon the selfishness of man's nature; opposition to it, on his love of justice."

CHAPTER V

DEFEAT OF THE LITTLE GIANT

LINCOLN had worked very hard in Illinois. All this year he was making speeches; educating the people of the State; helping them to understand the big questions before them; making things clear in his own mind by putting them into the clear and simple words that would carry their importance to the minds of others.

A great meeting was held, summoned by the editors of the newspapers that were against the Kansas Bill; they invited prominent men from different parts of the country to come and address them.

Lincoln was among those who went, and his speech was by far the most important of all that were delivered there. He had not, indeed, intended to say anything; but he was roused by the weakness of those who did address the meeting. Springing to his feet, he poured out what was in his mind, and could not be kept back, in such burning and eloquent words that the reporters dropped their pencils and listened spellbound. The whole audience was carried away by excitement: it was one of the greatest speeches that Lincoln ever made, we are told by all who heard it, but there is no record of it. Lincoln himself spoke in a transport of enthusiasm: the words came, how he hardly knew; he could not afterwards write down what he had said. The reporters were so deeply moved that they only took down a sentence here and there. The speech was a warning to the growing Republican party: sentences were quoted and remembered.

The North was indeed beginning to awaken to the need of uniting against slavery; but it took four years before it fully awoke. And as long as the North was divided the South was irresistible. When the presidential election came, in 1856, the votes of the South carried the day.

Had a strong man, with definite and wise views, been elected, had Lincoln been elected, the war between North and South that came four years later might have been prevented. But Lincoln's fame had not yet travelled far beyond Illinois; he was not

Springing to his feet, he poured out what was in his mind

DEFEAT OF THE LITTLE GIANT 59

even nominated. Mr. Buchanan, the new President, called himself a Democrat: he believed in Douglas's policy of State rights; but he was a tool in the hands of the South. Weak and undecided, his stupid administration made war inevitable. He did not satisfy the South; and he showed the North how great a danger they were in, so that when the next election came they were ready to act.

The Republican party gradually grew strong. More and more Northern voters came to see that its policy, no extension of slavery, was the only right one. The pro-slavery party in Kansas continued to behave in the most violent way; civil war continued.

In Congress, Charles Sumner made a number of eloquent speeches on what he called the "crime against Kansas"; and in them he openly attacked slavery. One day, as he was sitting in the members' reading-room, a Southern member called Brookes came in. Although there were several other people in the room, Brookes fell upon Sumner, and with his heavy walking-stick, which was weighted with lead at the end, beat him within an inch of his life. For the next four years Sumner was an invalid, and unable to take part in politics.

This incident caused great indignation in the North; their indignation was heightened by the attempt to force slavery on Kansas, till it grew in very many cases to a real hatred of slavery itself.

But there was still a large party in the North which did not disapprove of slavery. This party was led, of course, by Douglas. Douglas had been successful up till now, because he represented the ordinary man of the North, whose conscience was not yet awake, who did not see that slavery, in itself, was wrong. Lincoln had never really succeeded until now, because his conscience had always been awake, and the ordinary Northerner was not ready to follow him.

The whole question of slavery was brought under discussion in the next year—1857—by the famous case of a negro called Dred Scott. Dred Scott claimed his freedom before the United States courts, because his master, a doctor, had taken him to live in the free State of Illinois. The chief-justice—Taney—was an extreme pro-slavery man. He was not satisfied with deciding the case against Dred Scott; he went much further, and declared that since a negro is property and not a person in the legal sense, he could not bring a case before an American court. A negro, he declared, has no rights which a white man is bound to respect.

The South, of course, was delighted with this verdict. What it meant was this. When the Declaration of Independence declared that all men are equal, and possess right to life and liberty, what was intended was not all men, but all white men, since black men are not legally men. And yet free negroes had fought in the War of Independence, and signed the Declaration.

To the North such reasoning was hateful. People like Mr. Seward of New York began to say, If slavery is part of the Constitution of America, there is a law that is higher than the Constitution—the moral law. Abraham Lincoln in a noble speech declared: "In some respects the black woman is certainly not my equal, but in her natural right to eat the bread she earns with her own hands she is my equal, and the equal of all others." The point was, could a negro have rights? The Dred Scott decision declared "no," the South shouted "no." The Republican party said "yes." In this same year a free election at last took place in Kansas; and a huge majority decided that the State should not hold slaves.

All these events showed that troublous times were coming.

In the next year a set of speeches was made which showed people how things stood. In 1858 Lincoln stood against Douglas as candidate for the State of Illinois. Douglas was one of the most famous and popular men then living in America. He was far the cleverest man and the best speaker of his party; he stood for all those who, though they might not want to have slaves themselves, thought that slavery was not wrong; that black men were intended by a kind Providence to be useful to white men. If any State wanted slaves, let them have them —why not?

As Lincoln said, "Douglas is so put up by nature, that a lash upon his back would hurt him, but a lash upon anybody else's back does not hurt him."

Those who did not know Lincoln thought it absurd that he, an unknown man from the country, should dare to stand against Douglas, the "Little Giant." But Lincoln was not afraid; he did not think of himself; he wanted people to hear what he had to say. He arranged with Douglas that they should hold a number of meetings together in Illinois. They arranged it in this way. At half the

DEFEAT OF THE LITTLE GIANT

meetings Douglas spoke first for an hour; then Lincoln replied, speaking for an hour and a half, and Douglas answered him in half-an-hour's speech. At the other half, Lincoln began and Douglas followed, Lincoln ending.

You can imagine one of these meetings. A large hall, roughly built for the most part, the seats often made of planks laid on top of unhewn logs, packed with two or three thousand people, intensely eager to hear and learn. Some of them were already followers of Douglas, the most popular man in America: all of them had heard of the "Little Giant," the cleverest speaker in the States. Immense cheering as Douglas rose to his feet. A small man with a big head: a handsome face with quickly moving, keen, dark eyes; faultlessly dressed. A well-bred gentleman, secure of himself—a lawyer with all his art at the end of his tongue: able to persuade any one that black was white, to wrap up anything in so many charming words that only the cleverest could see when one statement did not follow from another, when an argument was not a proof: quick to see and stab the weak points in any one else. A voice rich and mellow, various and well trained, pleased all who heard it.

For an hour he spoke, amid complete silence, only broken by outbursts of applause. When he ended, there were deafening cheers —then a pause, and "Lincoln," "Lincoln," from all parts of the hall.

Lincoln seemed an awkward countryman beside the senator. His tall body seemed too big for the platform, and his ill-fitting black clothes hung loosely upon it, as if they had been made for some one else. When he began to speak his voice was harsh and shrill. His huge hands, the hands of a labourer, with the big knuckles and red, ugly wrists, got knotted together as if nothing could unfix them. Soon, however, he became absorbed in what he was saying; he ceased to be nervous; everything seemed to change. As he forgot himself, his body seemed to expand and straighten itself, so that every one else looked small and mean beside him; his voice became deep and clear, reaching to the farthest end of the hall, and his face, that had appeared ugly, was lit up with an inner light that made it more than beautiful. The deep grey eyes seemed to each man in the hall to be looking at him and piercing his soul. The language was so simple that the most ignorant man in the

DEFEAT OF THE LITTLE GIANT

hall could follow it and understand. Everything was clear. There was no hiding under fine words; nothing was left out, nothing unnecessary was said. No one could doubt what Lincoln meant; and he was not going to let any one doubt what Douglas meant.

The greatest debate of all was that at the meeting at Freeport. At Freeport Lincoln asked Douglas a question, against the advice of all his friends. He asked whether, if a State wanted not to have slavery, it could so decide? Lincoln knew that if Douglas said "No. A state which had slavery must keep it," the people of Illinois would not vote for him, and he would lose this election. If he said "yes" he would be elected, and not Lincoln. Lincoln knew this; he knew that if Douglas said "yes," he was safe, and he would say "yes."

"Where do you come in, then?" his friends asked him. "Why do you ask him this? If you do, Douglas is sure to get in. You are ruining your own chances."

"I do not come in anywhere," said Lincoln; "but that does not matter. What does matter is this. If Douglas says 'yes,' as he will, he will get into the Senate now; but two years after this he will stand for election as President. If he says 'yes' now, the South will vote against him then, and he will not be elected. He must not be elected. No one who believes in spreading slavery must be elected. It does not matter about me."

Lincoln was quite right. He saw further than any one else. Douglas said "yes," and he was elected for Illinois. But the Democratic party in the South, whose support had made him strong, began to distrust him. "Douglas," said Lincoln, "is followed by a crowd of blind men; I want to make some of these blind men see."

Lincoln was defeated, but he did not think of himself. His speeches against Douglas were printed and read all over America. He was invited to speak in Ohio; and in the next year, in the beginning of 1860, a society in New York asked him to come and give them an address on politics.

A huge audience, in which were all the best known and most brilliant men of the day, gathered to hear him; an audience very much unlike any that he had addressed before. They were all anxious to see what he was like—this backwoodsman and farm-labourer, who had met the great Stephen Arnold Douglas and proved a match for him in argument; whose speeches had been printed to express the views of a whole party.

His appearance was strange and impressive. When he stood up his height was astonishing, because his legs were very long, and when sitting he did not appear tall. His face, thin and marked by deep lines, was very sad. A mass of black hair was pushed back from his high forehead: his eyebrows were black too, and stood out in his pale face: his dark-grey eyes were set deep in his head. The mouth could smile, but now it was stern and sad. The face was unlike other faces: when he spoke it was beautiful, for he felt everything he said. Abraham Lincoln was a common man: he had had no advantages of birth, of training: he had known extreme poverty: for years he had struggled without success in mean and small occupations: he had no knowledge but what he had taught himself. But no one who heard him speak could think him common.

Speaking now to an audience in which were the cleverest people in New York, people who had read everything and seen everything and been everywhere, who had had every opportunity that he had not, he impressed them as much as he had impressed the people of Illinois. He was one of the greatest orators that ever lived. His words went straight to the people to whom they were spoken. What he said was as straightforward and as certain as a sum in arithmetic, as easy to follow: and behind it all you felt that the man believed every word of what he said, and spoke because he must. The truth was in him.

Lincoln's address in New York convinced the Republican party that here was the man they wanted.

In 1860 there came the presidential election, always the most important event in American politics; this year more important than ever before.

For the last half-century almost the Democratic party had been in power. They had been strong because they were united: they united the people of the South and those people in the North who thought that it was waste of time to discuss slavery, since slavery was part of the Constitution. Their policy on slavery had been to leave it alone. As long as they did this there was nothing to create another party in the North strong enough to oppose them. But when Douglas, in order to make his own position strong in the South, made slavery

DEFEAT OF THE LITTLE GIANT

practical politics by bringing in a bill to allow Kansas to have slaves; and when the judges in the Dred Scott case roused sympathy with the negroes by declaring that slaves were not men but property, then the question united the divided North into a strong Republican party in which all were agreed. There was to be no slavery north of Mason and Dixon's line. The attempt to force slavery on Kansas split the Democratic party. One section was led by Douglas, who had gone as far as he could: he was not ready to force Kansas to have slaves, if she did not want them, because people from Missouri wanted her to have them. He saw that to force slavery on the North in this way would mean division and war, and therefore he refused to go any further. By this refusal Douglas lost his supporters in the South. They joined the section led by Jefferson Davis—the Southern candidate for the presidentship.

Jefferson Davis was the true leader of the South. Douglas as well as Lincoln had begun life as the child of a poor pioneer: each had risen by his own abilities and by constant hard work. Jefferson Davis was a true aristocrat. He was the son of rich and educated parents. All his life he had been waited on by slaves and surrounded by every comfort. While Lincoln was ploughing or hewing wood, while Douglas was working hard at the bar, Davis went first to the university at Kentucky and then to the military academy at West Point, from which he passed to the army. He served as a lieutenant at the time of the Black Hawk war, and it is very likely that he came across Lincoln, who was serving as a volunteer. After serving seven years in the army he married and settled down as a cotton planter in Mississippi. His estates were worked by slaves, of course. To him the negro was an animal, quite different from the white man, meant by nature to be under him and to serve him. Black men, unlike white, did not exist for themselves, with the equal right to live possessed by a man, an insect, or a tree, but had been created solely to be useful to white men.

No two men could be more unlike than Lincoln and Davis. The groundwork of Davis' nature was an intense pride. A friend described him as "as ambitious as Lucifer and as cold as a lizard." He was cold in manner and seldom laughed. Lincoln was entirely humble-minded, full of passionate longing to help the weak. To Lincoln

DEFEAT OF THE LITTLE GIANT

what was common was therefore precious. Jefferson Davis said the minority, and not the majority, ought to rule. And their looks were as unlike as their minds. Jefferson Davis, with his beautiful proud face, as cold and as handsome as a statue, expressed the utter contempt and scorn of the aristocrat for everything and every one beneath him.

When the Democratic party met at Charleston to nominate their candidate for the presidentship, they were hopelessly divided. Douglas's Freeport speech had set the South against him. For the last four years there had been a growing section which said that, as long as the South was fastened to the North, slavery was not safe. Now seven states, led by South Carolina, left the Democratic meeting and nominated Davis as their candidate.

The Republican party met at Chicago. There was only one man strong, reasonable, and sane enough for every section of the party to accept. This was Abraham Lincoln. At the time of his nomination, Lincoln was playing barnball with his children in the field behind his house. When told that he had been chosen, he said, "You must be able to find some better man than me." But he was ready to take up the difficult task.

He knew that he could serve his country, and he was not afraid. He had a clear ideal before him — to preserve America as one united whole. He saw that war might come. As he had said, five years before, America could not endure for ever half slave and half free — it must be all free: and the South would not let slavery go without war.

The election came in November. The result was that Lincoln was elected President. For four years the destiny of his country was in his hands.

CHAPTER VI

THE NEW PRESIDENT AND SECESSION

LINCOLN'S election was a thunderbolt to the South. It meant that the great question of slavery would have to be decided one way or another. Lincoln was a man who had opinions, and opinions in which he believed, for which he would fight; he would not let things drift as Buchanan did. Buchanan's policy would have ended in allowing the South to separate itself from the North; the Southern politicians knew this, and they wanted Buchanan's policy carried on, so as to make that separation possible.

Few men in the North, although many in the South, understood as clearly as Lincoln did the position of affairs. He saw that the time had come when active measures must be taken, a strong and decided policy maintained, if the Union was to be held together. He was a true patriot.

He believed in the Union; he thought it a great and glorious thing. That North and South should be separated was to him like separating husband and wife; their strength and happiness lay in each other; they had grown together for eighty-four years; if they parted now, each must lose something it could never regain. He loved his country. He loved the South as well as the North. He believed that if the South tried to separate, the North would be justified, in the true interests of the American nation, in compelling her to remain.

The great problem was now, as he saw: Could America hold together as one nation, half slave and half free? Could the Union be a real Union while there was this deep division, a division which it was now clear could not be got rid of, as the Northerners had hoped for so long, by the slow passage of time? Time alone would not induce the South to give up slavery. Slavery was a barbarous institution, degrading to the slaves and to those who owned them; the North could not accept it. If North and South were to hold together slavery must go. The great thing was to keep North and South united. This and this only was Lincoln's great purpose. He

THE NEW PRESIDENT 75

hated slavery, but he would not have compelled the South to give up slavery if he had believed that the Union could have been maintained without that. North and South must hold together whatever it cost; only so could each part of the nation, and the nation as a whole, attain the best that was possible for it.

Lincoln's great difficulty was this. The South saw that the nation could not hold together for ever half slave and half free. Two years before Lincoln's election, one of the members for South Carolina had written what was afterwards known as the Scarlet Letter. In it he declared, "We can make a revolution in the cotton States," and there were many, even at that time, who shared his views. The South saw that, if they were to remain united to the North, slavery must go, and they were ready to separate from the North in order to keep slavery.

But, while the South understood the position, the North did not. It did not understand it fully at the time of Lincoln's election, or, indeed, until the end of the second year of the war. And because they did not understand they could not appreciate Lincoln's policy, or support it as they ought to have done. All the time they criticised, blamed, and abused him, making his hard task harder.

Not until after his death did all the Northerners see how great and how right he had been. Not until his death did Americans realise that had it not been for Lincoln the United States might have ceased to be.

Lincoln's speeches had been plain and outspoken enough; the South was terrified by his election. They resolved on separation.

Lincoln, though elected in November 1860, did not actually become President until February 1861. During these three months he remained in the plain, yellow house at Springfield, his little office crowded every day with visitors who came to consult him, to advise him, or often merely to shake his hand. "Honest old Abe," as they called him, had a joke or a kindly word for all of them. He was presented with many quaint gifts. An old woman came one day, and, after shaking hands with Lincoln, produced from under her huge cloak a vast pair of knitted stockings for the President to wear in winter. Lincoln thanked her graciously and led her out; then returning, he lifted

THE NEW PRESIDENT

up the stockings, and showing the enormous feet, said to his secretary, "The old lady seems to have guessed the latitude and longitude about right!"

Lincoln spent the time reading and writing, drawing up memoranda, choosing his Cabinet, learning the difficult ins and outs of the new work before him. All these months he was thinking hard. His purpose was already clear: but the presidentship, always a heavy burden, had never been so heavy as it was to be for Lincoln.

Things grew more serious every day. The weakness of Buchanan, who had no plan or purpose, allowed the South to do as it chose. The only chance of avoiding war lay in firm action now; but it was not in Buchanan's nature to be firm. He had been made President by the votes of the South because he was not firm, because he would allow them to do as they chose. They dreaded Lincoln because he was firm, and therefore acted while there was yet time.

On December 20, 1860, the chief men of South Carolina met together and declared the Union to be dissolved. Posters appeared all over the State: the South was in a state of feverish excitement. Within the month the States of Missouri, Alabama, Florida, Georgia, Louisiana, and Texas—the chief cotton-growing, slave-owning States—also declared themselves to be separated from the Union; and these six States joined with South Carolina to form what they called the Southern Confederation, independent of the North. They chose for their first President Jefferson Davis.

Buchanan did not know what to do. The question was: Has a State any right to leave the Union? America, of course, is a Federation: at the time of the Declaration of Independence the thirteen States that then existed joined themselves together for ever, and created a common Federal Government for common purposes, with a President at its head. Lincoln would have said one State has no more right to leave the others than an English county has to declare that it is a separate kingdom, not bound by the common law. Buchanan said "no," too; but he also said, if a State does leave, the Federal Government has no right to force it to stay: which meant a standstill. "You ought not to want to go; but if you do, we have no right to prevent you." Buchanan's one idea, indeed, was to let things drift.

THE NEW PRESIDENT 79

There was one great and immediate difficulty. In each of the coast States of the Union the Federal Government had armed forts: in South Carolina there were two important ones, Fort Moultrie and Fort Sumter, with a small garrison in each, commanded by Major Anderson. South Carolina demanded that the garrisons should be withdrawn. Now to withdraw the garrisons and abandon the forts was to admit that South Carolina had a right to leave the Union, and to recognise the Southern Confederation as independent of the Federal Government. To maintain the forts more forces must be sent. Anderson wrote to say that he was not strong enough to hold out against an attack. Buchanan did nothing. Anderson, believing that an attack was going to be made on Fort Moultrie, which he was too weak to defend, removed all his men to Fort Sumter. The militia of South Carolina at once occupied Fort Moultrie.

In the second week of the new year, 1861, a Government vessel, the *Star of the West*, sailed into the harbour of Charleston to bring provisions for Anderson. The *South Carolina*, having attacked the *Star of the West*, fired on the United States flag which it carried, and drove it out of the harbour. The Confederate Government, led by Jefferson Davis, then demanded that Fort Sumter should be given up to them. When Anderson refused, it was blockaded by much superior forces, and by the 12th of April it was taken by General Beauregard.

Under these circumstances, when war was at hand, when half the nation was ready to take up arms against the other half, Lincoln took up the burden of office. It was a burden, indeed, which no ordinary man could have borne. Buchanan had simply looked on while rebellion was preparing itself; for Lincoln was the task of quelling it. But the fact of rebellion was not his greatest difficulty. This was the disunion of the North. One section—the Abolitionists—rejoiced at the secession of the South. "We shall no more be chained to the slave-owners." Another section thought that, if the South wanted to go, why not let them.

There was as yet only a very small section able to agree with Lincoln. Lincoln hated slavery but not slave-owners. He loved the South as much as the North. It was agony to him to know his country divided against itself. Well might he say, in the speech he made on leaving his old home at Springfield

THE NEW PRESIDENT

for ever, "There is a task before me greater than that which rested upon Washington."

It was very natural that men who had not known Lincoln should fear to have the fate of their country at so critical a time entrusted to a man of so small experience. But any one who knew Lincoln felt absolute confidence in him. Years of difficulty and disappointment, of constant struggle against every kind of obstacle, had made him what he was: clear-eyed to see where the right was; steadfast and unflinching to pursue it; tender-hearted and generous to sympathise with all those who stumbled on the way.

Few people, indeed, understood him. In the years to come nearly all at one time or another abused him and distrusted him, and blamed him when things went wrong. For four years he bore the whole burden of a great responsibility; patiently and silently he endured disappointment and reproach. In the end he could say that if Washington had made America one, he had remade it so that it could never again be unmade.

The speech he made when he entered on his duties as President showed how little bitterness there was in his heart towards the South. He said, "We are not enemies, but friends. We must not be enemies. Though passion may have strained, it must not break, our bonds of affection. The mystic chords of memory, stretching from every battlefield and patriot grave to every heart and hearthstone all over this broad land, will yet swell the chorus of the Union when touched, as surely they will be, by the better angels of our nature."

The attack on Sumter and its fall made war inevitable. Lincoln was no Buchanan. War was horrible; civil war—war between men of the same country, between friends, often between relations—most horrible of all. But he could not, at whatever cost, allow the Union, for which his countrymen had fought so heroically eighty-four years ago, which had stood so long for such a high ideal of freedom all over the world—he could not allow the Union to be destroyed without fighting to preserve it. To him the secession of the Southern States meant something as unnatural as a separate kingdom in Scotland would be to us, and a kingdom based on something which we thought wholly wrong.

"The question is," he said, "whether in a free Government the minority have a right to break it up whenever they choose."

THE NEW PRESIDENT

He declared that they had no such right. The whole population of the slave-holding States was much smaller than that of the free States, and among those States, while seven had seceded, eight remained at least nominally in the Union; and even in the seceding States themselves, there was a party in each that was ready to remain faithful to the Union, and not prepared to take up arms against it.

They wanted war: their attack on Fort Sumter was a call to arms. They wanted war: they should have it. In the long run the North was bound to win: its population was half as great again, and its resources as much superior.

Almost the first act of Lincoln's Government was to call for 75,000 volunteers.

The attack upon Sumter and Lincoln's call to arms roused the North from its apathy. Excitement grew when the 7th Massachusetts regiment, passing through Baltimore on its way to headquarters, was violently attacked by the mob: when the Southern army, already in the field, captured Harper's Ferry and seized the Union arsenal at Gosport.

CHAPTER VII

THE WAR

WAR began in Virginia. West Virginia was free, East Virginia slave-holding; the State was the natural meeting-place for the two armies. On the 21st July they met at Bull Run: the engagement could hardly be called a battle—on neither side was there any order or discipline. More than once during the day the Southern army seemed to be beaten, but it rallied, and the Federalists, as the Union soldiers were called, broke into a disgraceful retreat, which became an awful panic. The fugitives poured into Washington, haggard and dust-stained: everything seemed lost. Lincoln did not go to bed all night; he paced up and down in his room, expecting that the victorious Confederate army would march upon Washington, and the war be at an end. It did not come. The opportunity was lost. A battle had been gained; that was all.

The moral effect of the battle of Bull Run was very great indeed. The South thought the war was over, the North saw that it had only begun.

At first, the Confederates seemed to have great advantages. The army was the one profession for a Southern gentleman; nearly all their young men were trained at the military academy at West Point, and a great many of the officers of the United States army had been Southerners. These men now left the Union army and gave their services to the Confederates; among them was General Robert Lee, who became General-in-Chief of the Confederate army. Lincoln's difficulties were greatly increased by the fact that so many officers and men went over to the Confederates. At the beginning, the South had a larger and better-trained army in the field; and at first there were plenty of volunteers. But after Bull Run, she thought the war was finished; and events proved that, in a long war, the North must win by reason of her greater staying power.

The South was as enthusiastic as the North, and at the beginning better prepared, but not equal in resources of any sort. The South was entirely dependent on agriculture; all the necessaries of life came from the North and from Europe. Whereas the South had to import all her ammunition, the North had powder-magazines of her own, and a people of mechanics. And the Confederacy was soon to find that men are useless without arms. Great sufferings were endured, wonderful invention and patience was shown, on both sides there was great heroism; but in the end the resources of the North decided the day.

Lincoln threw all his energy into the task of getting ready an army, and in a short time the Northern soldier was as well trained and equipped as the Southern.

The battle of Bull Run roused the North: quickened by shame, the people were ready to fight to the bitter end. For the next two years, however, they were disheartened by continual disaster: army after army was destroyed, position after position lost: gloom descended on the nation. In the dark times of defeat men turned upon Lincoln and blamed him for everything.

His position was difficult indeed. As head of the State, he was also commander of the army; but he had to entrust the actual management of the campaigns to others. He followed and understood their tactics, but was too wise to try to direct their movements. Only occasionally did he offer advice —wise advice, which his generals were not always wise enough to accept. At first the generals were not men of great ability. M'Clellan, the commander, drilled his army in a wonderful way, but never used it to any effect. In the Virginian campaign of 1861 and 1862 he threw away numberless opportunities. His place was taken by Burnside at the end of 1862; but not until the rise of Ulysses S. Grant did Lincoln discover a really great commander. The generals quarrelled with one another, and all were ready to complain of the President. Lincoln's difficulties were increased by the fact that many people, when they found that the North was not going to conquer immediately, said that the war was a mistake: the South ought to be allowed to go if it wanted to. Lincoln did not think it right to let the South go: and because to keep it was proving difficult, was never to him a reason for ceasing to do what he saw to be right.

The newspapers abused Lincoln because the war, instead of being finished in three months, seemed likely to last for years. For long his own Cabinet was hardly loyal to him: each member thought he could manage affairs better himself. Seward, who was Chief Secretary, thought Lincoln stupid, and was anxious to arrange everything; but as experience of his chief taught him he became Lincoln's devoted admirer. Chase the Treasurer plotted against him: Stanton the War Secretary openly declared that "things would go all right but for the imbecile at the head." Stanton had no sense of humour, and an ungovernable temper. He did not understand Lincoln at all for a long time: his jokes puzzled and annoyed him, and he used to jump up and down with rage. He did not see that to a man of a deeply melancholy nature like Lincoln, a dreamer and something of a poet, some outlet, some way of escaping from himself, was necessary. Lincoln was marvellously patient with Stanton, and won his deep affection. The Cabinet might criticise; but Lincoln's firm will dominated them all. The policy of the Government was the President's policy.

No quality is so hard to appreciate, until it succeeds, as patience; and for two years Lincoln was patient, and few understood.

England and France were inclined to recognise the Confederacy. The English point of view was not one which reflected any glory on the nation. Lord Palmerston said, "We do not like slavery, but we want cotton." And a poem in *Punch* expressed the general point of view, against which only a few Englishmen protested—

> "Though with the North we sympathise,
>   It must not be forgotten
> That with the South we've stronger ties,
>   Which are composed of cotton,
> Whereof our imports mount unto
>   A sum of many figures;
> And where would be our calico
>   But for the toil of niggers?"

France agreed with England. Under such circumstances there was a great danger that, unless the North proved itself able to cope with the Rebellion, England or France might send help to the Confederates. For two years the North did not prove this; for two years it seemed, except to the very far-seeing, almost certain that the South would win.

The Northern plan of campaign was to attack and close round the Confederacy: to do this it was necessary to cross the

Potomac river, and clear away the Southern armies that blockaded it. The Potomac was the centre of operations, while fighting went on constantly in Virginia and Missouri. Everything went against the North.

On the 9th of August a desperate encounter took place at Wilson's Creek, at which the Union army lost nearly two thousand men, including prisoners, and large supplies of arms and ammunition. In September the Confederates won a victory at Lexington, and in October the Federal troops were defeated at Ball's Bluff.

Lincoln's plan was gradually to shut the South in, driving it behind its own boundaries by means of the armies invading from north and west, and blockading the ports from the sea. So far the first half of the plan was not successful. But the Civil War was won to a very large extent by the Northern navy. By blockading the Southern ports it prevented the South from getting supplies from Europe; and since the South depended for supplies of every sort from abroad, it was in a desperate position when cut off from the sea.

More fortunate on sea than on land, Lincoln found in David Farragut an admiral almost as great as Nelson. Farragut was a Southerner by birth, but he had served for fifty years in the United States navy, and refused to desert it now. Patriotism to him meant devotion not to the pride but to the best interests of his country, and he thought that North and South could only attain their best interests when united. In April the Northern army suffered a severe defeat on land at the battle of Shiloh—the most disastrous yet experienced; but the news was balanced by the tidings of Farragut's capture of New Orleans. The fighting in the harbour was tremendous.

"Don't flinch from that fire, boys," cried the admiral; "there is a hotter fire for those who don't do their duty!"

Inspired by his example, his men did not flinch, and the town was captured. The North needed all the encouragement such naval victory could give it, for things were going very badly. Stonewall Jackson, the Southern commander, carried everything before him in Virginia. Washington was in danger; there was a panic in the capital. Jackson, however, did not want to attack

Washington. His plan was to compel M'Clellan, who was slowly moving south to attack the Confederate capital at Richmond, to turn north again.

There was fighting all through June; Jackson had been joined by Lee, the Confederate Commander-in-Chief. On the 1st of July a battle was fought at Malvern Hill. Lee and Jackson were defeated. M'Clellan ought now to have pushed on to Richmond, the Confederate capital, instead of which, with extraordinary stupidity, he continued to retreat.

In August, the second battle of Bull Run resulted in another victory for the South. Both sides lost an extraordinary number of men. The panic in Washington grew more acute when, early in September, Lee prepared to invade Maryland. M'Clellan again delayed when he ought to have forced an engagement. The people of Maryland received the Southern army very coldly. On the 17th the armies met at Antietam. The battle was not really decisive; the losses of the North were as great as those of the South; but it put an end to their invasion. Lee recrossed the Potomac River to Virginia. M'Clellan again wasted time. He waited six weeks before pursuing Lee. In November M'Clellan was at last superseded.

Events had gradually led Lincoln to see the necessity of taking one great step—the freeing of the slaves. The question of slavery was at the bottom of the war; it was the great division between North and South. Two reasons led Lincoln to take this step now. One was that he knew the negroes when free would fight, for the most part, for the North; and the North needed every help she could find. The other was the great difficulty of knowing what to do with the negro slaves which fell into the hands of the conquerors of any part of Southern territory. On the 22nd of September, very soon after the news of the battle of Antietam and Lee's retreat from Maryland had arrived, Lincoln called a meeting of his Cabinet. None of them knew why he had summoned them.

They found the President reading Artemus Ward; one story amused him so much that he read it aloud. They all laughed a great deal except Stanton, who could never see a joke, and did not understand that Lincoln must have broken down altogether under the fearful strain of all he had to bear, if he had not been able sometimes to forget himself. When he had finished reading the story, the President's face grew grave again. He drew from his pocket a large sheet of foolscap, covered with his straight, regular writing, and read it to the Cabinet.

It was the Emancipation Proclamation, which declared that, after January 1st of the coming year, all slaves were to be free; that Government would pay some compensation to loyal owners. No one dared oppose Lincoln when his mind was made up. His reason for introducing Emancipation now was, that he thought it would help the cause of Union, and that cause was to him sacred beyond everything. "As long as I am President," he said later, "this war shall be carried on for the sole purpose of restoring the Union. But no human power can subdue this rebellion without the use of the Emancipation policy."

His first object in everything was to hold the American nation together as one whole. But, at the same time, he de-

Lincoln reading the Emancipation Proclamation to his Cabinet

tested slavery as much as any man. "If slavery is not wrong, nothing is wrong." An opportunity had now come when to strike a blow at slavery was to assist the Union cause. By freeing the blacks, Lincoln provided the North with a new resource, at the time when the South had nowhere to turn to for fresh resources. By declaring the abolition of slavery an unchangeable part of the Union, which the South must accept before peace could be made, he won the sympathy of Europe for the North, and prevented it from sending help to the South at a time when such help would have changed the balance of affairs.

Up till now both England and France had shown themselves ready to sympathise with the South. English newspapers abused Lincoln and the North in the most violent language. In the English dockyards vessels had been built and equipped which were used by the South as privateers to do great damage to the Northern navy. One of these was the famous *Alabama*. But when the war was a war against slavery, English feeling was all on the side of the North.

The United States was made a really free

country: slavery, which had made such a name a mockery, was wiped off the statute book.

Lincoln showed rare judgment and courage in doing what he did at this time. At first a large section in the North was opposed to Emancipation, but gradually all united in admiring the wisdom of Lincoln's action. The South knew that if they were conquered slavery was gone. And however black things might look, Lincoln and the North were not going to give in till they did conquer. They had set their teeth; they were going to fight to the bitter end.

M'Clellan had been dismissed, but his successors were not much more successful. In December Burnside threw away thousands of lives in an attempt to scale Mary's Heights. Men were shot down in heaps by the enemy, and the army fell into a panic; a battle against overwhelming odds ended in a complete defeat. Lincoln's heart bled for the loss of so many splendid citizens: there was deep indignation in Washington, much of it vented against the President.

The darkest moment of the war came when, in May, the news of the battle of

Chancellorsville reached the Government. Hooker met Jackson: a long and fearfully bloody battle followed. There were dreadful losses on both sides: another valuable opportunity of pressing south was lost. In the battle "Stonewall" Jackson was killed, shot accidentally by his own men; a disastrous loss to the Southern side, though the North was defeated.

All hope seemed gone from the North.

Up till now the North had lost more than the South. It had suffered most of all from a lack of really able commanders. Now, however, Lincoln discovered a really great general in Ulysses S. Grant, and from this time on the fortune of the war began to change.

The North was richer: it had more men, money, and resources to draw on; in a long struggle the South was bound to be worn out. Grant saw this and planned accordingly. Grant had distinguished himself early in the war by the capture of Fort Henry and Fort Donelson, on the Mississippi, in February 1862; in the following April he had driven the Confederates back to Corinth after one of the most expensive battles of the war. Grant was a man of the most reckless personal courage; as a general his great fault was that he exposed his men needlessly. Complaints were early made of him to Lincoln; but Lincoln's wonderful eye discerned a great soldier in Grant. "I can't spare that man; he fights." Later he was told that Grant drank. "Pray tell me what brand of whisky he takes, that I may send a barrel to each of my other generals."

Lincoln and Grant always understood each other. Each was a man of intense strength of character, given to doing things rather than talking of them. Grant had not Lincoln's tenderness of heart, or the beauty of his pure and generous nature; but he had his power of concentrating his whole mind upon the task in hand. He knew Lincoln's secret: "Work, work, is the main thing."

The battle of Chancellorsville, May 1863, was for the North the darkest moment of the war; things were never so dark again. Only Lincoln's supreme faith and courage could have risen from such a series of defeats unshaken. The newspapers were full of abuse of the President; plots were on foot against him to prevent his re-election when the time came. In February he had lost his son Willie after a long and painful illness. But he never quailed.

And his patience was at last to be rewarded. After Chancellorsville his unflinching belief in the justice of his course, in spite of opposition and discontent, was to be rewarded: he was to look, if only for a moment, upon an America not only free but united.

CHAPTER VIII

VICTORY

AFTER Chancellorsville the South thought that all was won, and a movement was set on foot to attack Washington. Lee marched north with an army that, though only half fed, was full of enthusiasm, and on July 1 took up his position at Gettysburg, where he was faced by the Federal army under General Meade. The battle lasted three days, and the slaughter was terrific; in spite of the desperate determination of the Confederates, the day ended in a victory for the Union.

Lee was driven back, and forced to retreat into Virginia. The invasion was at an end. The victory, though brilliant, was not followed up, perhaps because of the heavy losses of the Union army; but it was the turning-point of the war. Washington was never again in such danger; the Confederates had lost the one great opportunity of attack since Bull Run.

Deep national thankfulness was felt at this, the first great victory for the North. The battle-field was only a few miles from the capital, and many of the citizens and the most prominent men of the town assembled to perform a service for the dead who had fallen there. Lincoln was called upon to speak. He had not prepared anything, but the short speech which he gave made a deep impression upon all who heard it, and puts into very noble words the thoughts that were always present to his mind.

"Fourscore and seven years ago, our fathers brought forth a new nation upon this continent, conceived in liberty and dedicated to the proposition that all men are created equal. Now we are engaged in a great civil war, testing whether that nation, or any nation so conceived and so dedicated, can long endure. We meet to dedicate a portion of it as a final resting-place of those who here gave their lives that the nation might live. It is altogether fitting and proper that we should do this. But, in a larger sense, we cannot dedicate, we cannot consecrate, we cannot hallow this ground.

The brave men, living and dead, who struggled here, have consecrated it far above our power to add or detract. The world will take little note, nor long remember, what we say here, but it can never forget what they did here. It is for us, the living, rather to be dedicated here to the unfinished work that they have thus far so nobly carried on. It is rather for us to be dedicated here to the great task remaining before us: that from these honoured dead we take increased devotion for the cause for which they here gave the last full measure of devotion; that we here highly resolve that these dead shall not have died in vain; that this nation shall, under God, have a new birth of freedom, and that the government of the people, by the people, and for the people, shall not perish from the earth."

In words like these, Lincoln inspired the people of the North to see the greatness of the cause for which they were fighting; they were fighting for liberty, for a free government of free men, for a United America that might be to the world a pattern of such a free government. If the South won, if America were a house divided for ever against itself, one half would have slavery; if the North won, and America were a whole again, slavery was gone; the Declaration of Independence, proclaiming the equal rights of all men to life and liberty, would be for the first time fully realised.

And encouragement came at last. On the Fourth of July, on Independence Day, Grant telegraphed to Lincoln the news of the capture of Vicksburg. In the beginning of May Grant had defeated Pemberton, the Confederate general, and shut him up in the town with his great army. After an unsuccessful assault in the end of May, he sat down patiently before the town, prepared to wear out its resistance. After great sufferings, the famishing garrison surrendered; Pemberton and 30,000 men, whom the South could but ill spare, were prisoners of war. Hundreds of cannon and thousands of muskets fell into the victor's hands. Vicksburg was a position of importance, the key to the Mississippi. Lincoln could now say, "The Father of Waters again goes unvexed to the sea."

The joy in the North over these two victories was intense. The drooping spirits began to rise again; and as things went better, men turned with new confidence to the patient man whose courage had never failed him. With renewed spirit the North set itself to the great task before it.

Lincoln now had men who were able to carry out great designs. By the end of 1863 things looked hopeful. The army had a nucleus of veterans who had received the best possible training, and a set of generals whose positions had been won not by political influence, but by hard work. Grant, Sherman, and Sheridan were men of ability, experience, and power.

The plan of campaign for 1864, drawn up, under Lincoln's advice, by Grant and Sherman, was masterly; carried out magnificently, it led to the complete triumph of the North. It was the complete development of Lincoln's earlier plans. Grant, with the army of the west, was to face Lee in Virginia and drive him south; finally, to capture Richmond, the Confederate headquarters, and force Lee to yield. Sherman, marching south and east, was to carry the war into the heart of the Confederacy; to follow General Johnson, push him to the sea, and capture him. "We intend," said Sherman, "to fight Joseph Johnson till he is

Lincoln discussing the plan of campaign with General Grant

satisfied." Then Sherman, marching north, was to co-operate with Grant by cutting off Lee's retreat. Meantime Sheridan was to deal with General Early in the Shenandoah valley, west and south of Washington.

By May 1864 Grant crossed the Potomac and entered the wild district, full of hills and woods and undergrowth, known as the Wilderness, where the Union armies had suffered so many defeats. Grant saw that the only thing was to wear the Southern army out by hard fighting; and he fought hard all summer. He lost some thirty thousand men in the Wilderness. His policy was to bear so continuously on the enemy that they, having fewer men, and less possibility of recruiting, must be worn out. Slowly, with an immense loss of life on both sides, Grant forced Lee south.

Sherman meantime was fighting his way to Georgia. His task was as difficult as Grant's. The country was wild, and well adapted for concealing the enemy. It was impossible for him to communicate with the rest of the army.

After an expedition into Alabama, Sherman started on his "March to the Sea." Johnson disputed every inch of the way.

There was incessant skirmishing, but Sherman advanced step by step.

While Sherman and Grant were thus slowly wearing down the resistance of the enemy, the Unionists were once more encouraged by a brilliant naval success. In August Farragut came victorious out of a terrific fight in Mobile Bay. Entering the harbour in spite of the line of mines, he "plucked victory out of the very jaws of defeat."

Sherman was now besieging Atlanta, which he captured on September 1. About the same date Sheridan defeated Early at Winchester in the Shenandoah Valley.

These successes decided the presidential election. Lincoln had been unanimously nominated as the Republican candidate, "not," as he said, "because they have decided I am the greatest or best man in America, but rather they have concluded that it is not wise to swop horses while crossing a river, and have further concluded that I am not so poor a horse that they might not make a botch of it in trying to swop." Against him the Democratic party, whose main principle was opposition to the war, supported ex-General M'Clellan, declaring "the war is a failure." The Democrats found their main supporters among those (and they were fairly numerous) who disliked Lincoln's Emancipation proclamation.

Lincoln made no efforts to secure his re-election. He had been before the nation as President for four years: his policy was tried, his opinions known. Even M'Clellan did not dare to propose to abandon the Union. On that point the North was now united, and that being so the successes of September made Lincoln's re-election practically certain. Out of 233 electoral votes Lincoln received 212; he had a majority in every free State save one. The election was a complete triumph for the President.

The noble words of the address which he delivered on taking up his duties for a second time mark the spirit in which he celebrated that triumph. "With malice toward none; with charity for all; with firmness in the right as God gives us to see the right, let us strive on to finish the work we are in: to bind up the nation's wounds; to care for him who shall have borne the battle, and for his widow and his orphan — to do all that may achieve and cherish a just and lasting peace among ourselves and with all nations."

On November 16 Sherman marched on by Atlanta. By December he had reached Savannah and began to bombard the city. It surrendered on December 21, and Sherman wrote to Lincoln: "I beg to present to you, as a Christmas gift, the city of Savannah." Leaving Savannah early in the New Year, 1865, the army marched, ravaging, through South Carolina. Columbia was burned and Charleston captured. By March, Sherman was in North Carolina and in communication with Grant. The net was ready to be drawn round the Confederate army.

Grant meantime was bearing steadily on. The losses of the Union armies were enormous, and made the President's tender heart bleed. Grant began to be hampered by the inferior quality of his troops, and during the summer months matters seemed to be going ill with the North. In September, however, Sheridan inflicted a series of defeats upon Early in the Shenandoah Valley, and on October 18 vanquished him decisively at Cedar Creek.

The remaining Confederate army, under

VICTORY

Hood, was defeated at Nashville in the West, and now Lee's was the only army in the field. The Confederacy was "surrounded by a band of fire." The sea was in the hands of the Union; the Mississippi shut off any help from the coast. Sherman had harried Georgia and Carolina, destroying their supplies; Sheridan had raided Virginia; Grant was at the gates of Richmond.

Through the whole summer of 1864 and the winter of 1865 Grant besieged Richmond. There were indecisive engagements, but the armies did no more than "feel" each other. With the spring, however, Grant took the offensive again. On March 31 Sheridan gained a brilliant victory at Five Forks, and this enabled Grant to break Lee's lines. On April 3 the Stars and Stripes floated over Richmond. On April 9 Lee and his army surrendered to Grant at Appomatox.

The war was at an end.

Lincoln had been with Grant's army during the closing days of March; he entered Richmond on April 3. Everywhere the negroes saluted him as their liberator, kneeling on the ground before him and clasping his knees: "May de Lawd bress and keep you, Massa Presidum Linkum."

CHAPTER IX

"O CAPTAIN! MY CAPTAIN!"

NO one had suffered more deeply during the war than the President. His purpose never faltered. Even at the moment when success seemed farthest distant, his resolve stood firm; cost what it might the Union must be preserved. When almost every other man despaired of the Northern cause, Lincoln's invincible faith in the right and justice of their purpose sustained his country.

To attain that purpose thousands of lives had to be sacrificed; but the purpose was worth the loss of thousands of lives. Yet Lincoln's heart bled for every one of them.

All day long he received visits from distracted relations, mothers and wives asking him to pardon their sons or hus-

Lincoln visited all the divisions of his army in turn

bands in prison as deserters or captured from the enemy; asking for tidings of their beloved ones at the front. His generals complained that he undermined the discipline of the army by pardoning what he called his "leg" cases—cases where men had run away before the enemy. "If Almighty God gives a man a cowardly pair of legs, how can he help their running away with him?" said Lincoln.

The story of William Scott is a case which shows the way in which Lincoln used to act. William Scott was a young boy from a Northern farm, who, after marching for forty-eight hours without sleep, offered to stand on guard duty for a sick comrade. Worn out, he fell asleep, and was condemned to be shot for being asleep on duty in face of the enemy. Lincoln made it his custom to visit all the divisions of his army in turns, and, as it happened, two days before the execution he was with the division in which Willie Scott was, and heard of the case. He went to see the boy, and talked to him about his home and his mother. As he was leaving the prison tent he put his hands on the lad's shoulders, and said—

"My boy, you are not going to be shot to-morrow. . . . I am going to trust you and send you back to your regiment. But I have been put to a great deal of trouble on your account. I have come here from Washington, where I had a great deal to do. Now, what I want to know is, how are you going to pay my bill?"

Willie did not know what to say: perhaps he could get his friends to help him, he said at last.

"No," said Lincoln, "friends cannot pay it; only one man in the world can pay it, and that is William Scott. If from this day on William Scott does his duty, my bill is paid."

William Scott never forgot these words. Just before his death in one of the later battles of the war, he asked his comrades to tell President Lincoln that he had never forgotten what he had said.

All the time, people who did not know the President threw on his shoulders all the blame for the long continuance of the war. Until the last year of the war, the newspapers abused him continually. The horrible loss of life in Grant's last campaign was laid to

"O CAPTAIN! MY CAPTAIN!"

his charge. Only those who came to the President to ask his help in their own suffering, understood what his suffering was; he suffered with each of them—he suffered with the South as well as the North. After Antietam, he had said, "I shall not live to see the end; this war is killing me." The crushing burden he had borne so long and patiently had bent even his strong shoulders.

But it had not been borne in vain. The time seemed at last to have come when all America would understand how much they owed to the patient endurance of the President. And there was work still to be done which needed all his wisdom. The South was conquered. It had to be made one with the North. The pride of the conquerors had to be curbed, the bitterness of the conquered softened.

Lincoln returned from Richmond to Washington, in his heart the profound resolve "to bind up the nation's wounds" as he, and only he, could do it.

April 14 was Good Friday, and a day of deep thankfulness in the North. In the morning Lincoln held a Cabinet meeting, at which General Grant was present. The question of reconstruction, of making one whole out of the divided halves, was discussed. Some of the Cabinet were anxious to wreak vengeance on the South, to execute the leaders of the rebellion. Such was not Lincoln's view.

"Enough lives have been sacrificed. We must extinguish our resentments if we expect harmony and union."

His noble patriotism could still say to the South, "We are not enemies, but friends." His life was now even more precious to the South than to the North.

After the Cabinet meeting, Lincoln spent some time in talking with his son Robert, who had returned from the field with General Grant, under whom he had served as a captain. In the afternoon he went for a drive with Mrs. Lincoln. His mood was calm and happy: for the first time for four years he could look forward peacefully to the future, and to the great tasks still before him.

In the evening he went to the theatre with his wife and two young friends: the play was "Our American Cousin." The President was fond of the theatre—it was one of his few recreations: his appearance on this night was something of a public ceremony; therefore, although he was tired when evening came, he went because he knew that many people would be disappointed if he did not. The President had a box to the left of the stage. Suddenly, about the middle of the last act, a man appeared at the back of the box, a knife in one hand and a pistol in the other, put the pistol to the President's head and fired; then wounding Major Rathbone, the only other man in the box, with his knife, he vaulted on to the stage. As he leapt his spur caught the flag hanging from the box and he fell, breaking his leg. Nevertheless he rose instantly, and brandishing his knife and crying, "*Sic semper tyrannis!*" —"The South is avenged!" fled across the stage and out of sight.

The horrified audience was thunderstruck. The President lay quite still: the bullet had passed right through his head. The wound was mortal. He was carried to a house across the street, where he lay, quite unconscious, till the morning, surrounded by his friends, their faces as pale and haggard as his own. About seven, "a look of unspeakable peace came upon his worn features." Stanton, the War Secretary, rose from his knees by his side, saying, "Now he belongs to the ages."

There was profound sorrow through the whole of America; sorrow that checked all rejoicings over the victory of the North. Thus, indirectly, Lincoln's death helped the reconciliation between North and South, though nothing could counterbalance the loss of his wise guidance.

Washington was shrouded in black: even the poorest inhabitants showing their sorrow in their dress. The body was taken to Springfield, Illinois, to be buried; and all the towns on the way showed their deep mourning and respect. Now, and not till now, did Americans begin to understand what a man they had lost.

> "He knew to bide his time,
>   And can his fame abide,
> Still patient in his simple faith sublime
>   Till the wise years decide.
> Great captains with their guns and drums
>   Disturb our judgment for the hour,
> But at last silence comes:
>   These all are gone, and, standing like a tower,
> Our children shall behold his fame,
> The kindly, earnest, brave, far-seeing man,
> Sagacious, patient, dreading praise, not blame,
> New birth of our new soil, the first American."

"O CAPTAIN! MY CAPTAIN!"

So James Russell Lowell wrote of Lincoln when the celebration of Independence Day in the year of his death revived the vivid sense of loss.

The passage of years have only made clearer how great he was. Perfectly simple, perfectly sincere, he thought out for himself an ideal, and spent the whole of his life and all his strength in pursuing it.

He loved America, not because it was powerful and strong, but because it had been based on a great idea—the idea of liberty: his work for America was to realise that idea. He never thought of his own personal success: he wanted to be President because he saw a great work to be done and believed that he could do it. He never became rich: his own tastes remained entirely simple. He was said to have worn the same top-hat all his life.

The first thing that struck any one about Lincoln was his extraordinary appearance. He always dressed in black, with a big black tie, very often untied, or in the wrong place: his clothes looked as if they had been made to fit some one else, and had never been new. His feet were enormous; so were his hands, covered on state occasions with white kid gloves.

In cold weather he used to wear a large grey shawl instead of an overcoat. One day, before he was made President, some friends were discussing Lincoln and Douglas, and comparing their heights. When Lincoln came into the room some one asked him, "How long ought a man's legs to be?"

"Long enough to reach from his body to the ground," said Lincoln coolly.

Lincoln might look uncouth or even grotesque, but he did not look weak: he was the most striking figure wherever he went. No one who saw him often, no one who went to him in trouble, or to ask his advice, thought long of his appearance. Those who had once felt the sympathy of his wonderful, sad eyes, thought of that only. Those who really knew him, knew him to be the best man they had ever met.

Lincoln was often profoundly sad, and then suddenly boisterously gay. He enjoyed a joke or a funny story immensely: he often used to shock thoughtless people by telling some comic story on what they thought an unsuitable occasion; but he told it so well that however much they might disapprove they were generally forced to laugh.

Always rather a dreamer, he was fond of poetry. He knew long passages of Shakespeare by heart, especially Hamlet, Macbeth, and Richard III. The Bible he had known from his childhood; of Burns he was very fond.

Lincoln's rise to power, as even so short an account as this will have shown you, was not due to any extraordinary good fortune or any advantages at start. He taught himself all that he knew; he made himself what he was.

It was his character more than anything else that made him great. His early struggles had taught him that self-reliance which enabled him to persevere in a course which he thought right in spite of opposition, disloyalty, and abuse; they taught him the toleration which made him slow to judge others, generous to praise them, little apt to expect them to understand or praise him. He stood alone.

Not till he had gone did his people realise

how much he had given them; how much they had lost in him. He gave them, indeed, the most priceless gift a patriot can give his country—the example of sincere, devoted, and unselfish service.

THE END

Printed by BALLANTYNE, HANSON & Co.
Edinburgh & London

CPSIA information can be obtained
at www.ICGtesting.com
Printed in the USA
BVHW060034100920
588456BV00003B/179